SOLVING THE MYSTERY OF MENOPAUSE

SOLVING THE MYSTERY OF MENOPAUSE

WTH is happening to ME?

Angela Martinez, RN

NAPLES, FL

Copyright © 2024 by Angela Martinez
All rights reserved.

Published in the United States by
O'Leary Publishing
www.olearypublishing.com

The views, information, or opinions expressed in this book are solely those of the authors involved and do not necessarily represent those of O'Leary Publishing, LLC.

The author has made every effort possible to ensure the accuracy of the information presented in this book. However, the information herein is sold without warranty, either expressed or implied. Neither the author, publisher, nor any dealer or distributor of this book will be held liable for any damages caused either directly or indirectly by the instructions or information contained in this book. You are encouraged to seek professional advice before taking any action mentioned herein.

All rights reserved. No part of this book may be reproduced or transmitted in any form by any means, electronic, mechanical, photocopy, recording, or other without the prior and express written permission of the author, except for brief cited quotes.

For information on wholesale orders or getting permission for reprints and excerpts, contact: O'Leary Publishing at admin@olearypublishing.com

ISBN: 978-1-952491-78-8 (print)
ISBN: 978-1-952491-79-5 (ebook)
Library of Congress Control Number: 2023923970

Developmental Editing by Heather Davis Desrocher
Line Editing by Amber Chapman
Proofreading by Kat Langenheim
Cover and interior design by Jessica Angerstein

Printed in the United States of America

To all the women around the world,
Let my words be your voice as you navigate menopause.
May my story serve as a companion,
offering wisdom, hope, and even laughter
during times of uncertainty.

To my husband Jay,
I owe everything to you.
You have weathered the storm
with me every step of the way.
Without your love and understanding,
I would have gone off the deep end.
Thank you for keeping me grounded!

CONTENTS

Foreword A Husband's Perspective 1

Preface In the Dark, but Not Alone 7

PART 1: PERSONAL MENOPAUSE 13

  1 Facing the Truth 15

  2 You Are Not Alone 33

  3 Let's Talk About It 43

  4 Let's Have Some Fun 57

PART 2: PHYSICAL MENOPAUSE 69

  5 A Rollercoaster Ride of Hormones 71

  6 Hot . . . but Not 89

  7 The Toilet Diaries 99

  8 Treat Yourself 109

PART 3: MENTAL MENOPAUSE 121

  9 You Are Stressed, Now What? 123

  10 You Are NOT Crazy 137

  11 You're So/Still Sexy 145

  12 Embracing the Crone and Her Wisdom 155

Acknowledgments 167

About the Author 169

A HUSBAND'S PERSPECTIVE
by JAY MARTINEZ, PHARMD.

My first experience with menopause was when I was a boy. One afternoon, my sister and I were in the car with my grandparents driving around town hunting for doughnuts. Grandpa was in the driver's seat and Grandma was next to him. We were on one of those busy roadways with a stoplight at every block and Grandpa went through a few of those *yellowish* lights a bit quickly, and Grandma suddenly exploded. She yelled, "Stop the car!" right at an intersection. Keep in mind, traffic was everywhere, two lanes each way, with a median in the middle. Grandpa did stop the car. Then Grandma got out, slammed the door, and walked to the median with traffic moving both ways. Many angry words flew out of Grandma's mouth as Grandpa just sat there hoping she would come back. My sister and I were in the back seat with no clue what to do – so we froze.

Everything turned out fine. Grandma did get back in the car after Grandpa pleaded with her, and we drove off to get those doughnuts. And *that* was my first experience with menopause. My mom later explained what Grandma was going through, and why Grandpa ended up at our house sometimes needing a break on multiple occasions. That was menopause to my young mind. Grandma's reaction impacted me throughout my pharmacy education and marriage. I thought that is what menopause was going to be like for everyone.

Forty years later I found myself married to a woman who was going through menopause. I often wondered to myself, will she act just like Grandma and will I react just like Grandpa, wanting to run away and hide? Fortunately, my wife and I actually talk about things. We endured this together: night sweats, awake at night feeling on fire from her feet up to her head – sometimes 30 times a night! I did not want to see my wife suffer as my grandma did.

I have enjoyed my career as a pharmacist for 30 plus years. Our education includes anatomy and physiology of women's health. Did that give me enough understanding of what a woman goes through in this phase of her life? What she feels – what she fears? I wish that I could say that all my studies and experience as a pharmacist prepared me to help my wife through this journey. But to be honest, I was just as lost as anyone. My head knew what to do, my heart wanted to do something, but I kept thinking, "What do I do?" Did I truly understand her feelings? Did I realize that she felt powerless and exhausted, as if she was having a nervous breakdown?

As my wife navigated menopause, I am grateful she included me in her journey. We shared with each other more about ourselves than ever before. It resulted in a much better understanding of her difficulties through this phase of life, the physical changes that accompany menopause, and the mental awareness needed to make us stronger together. It was a wild ride, but one that I would do again because it taught me how to support her, and how not to be afraid.

In this book, Angela shares with you her menopause story: her experiences along the way, the research, how she felt, the pitfalls, and the successes. I urge you to use this book as a starting point for your own journey. Read it, share it with your loved ones, and let them partner with you along the way. You don't have to go through this alone.

Jay Martinez, PharmD.
Angela's Loving Husband

This information is not intended to diagnose,

treat, cure or prevent any disease.

PREFACE

IN THE DARK, BUT NOT ALONE

When I was 41 years old, I almost went under the knife for a hysterectomy at the recommendation of my gynecologist. Luckily, I did my own research and realized that having my uterus yanked out of me was not in my best interest, as I would have been completely unprepared for menopause at such an early age. I had originally met with my gynecologist because my monthly menstrual cycle was incredibly painful. I had been diagnosed with endometriosis in my 30s and had undergone several different treatment options for my pain. They were either short-lived or did not help me at all. I would then find myself going back to the doctor where he would suggest yet another procedure or want to prescribe another medication that I would not fill.

Eventually, my doctor suggested that I have a hysterectomy. He said that this was the only treatment that would help alleviate my pain. I discussed it with my husband and I talked to many women that had gone through this procedure. I received mixed reviews. Some women stated that having a hysterectomy was the best thing that they ever did. Others were not pleased with the procedure due to immediately experiencing menopause if their ovaries were also removed. I asked my doctor at my next appointment if he was going to take my ovaries as well. He stated yes, that my menstrual pain was occurring during ovulation and that they would need to be taken out if my goal was to be pain free. I then asked him about experiencing menopause. He said that it was more than likely that I would, but it would not affect me in a negative way. He never educated me on any of the lingering effects of the surgery – such as menopause.

I had to do a lot of thinking and research to answer so many of my unanswered questions. I decided to cancel my surgery and continue with the pain until I went into menopause naturally. I could not understand how my

PREFACE

gynecologist of 11 years did not sit down and talk to me about this possibility. That experience, along with my current trials of menopause, prompted me to write this book to prevent other women from suffering needlessly as I did.

HOW TO
USE THIS BOOK

This book is a guide that will help you, or your loved one, navigate this stage of life. This book is about perimenopause and menopause, and the three areas of a woman's life that it impacts: the personal, the physical, and the mental.

It is therefore broken into three parts.

I hope that you will find this book informative and a source of strength.

PART I
PERSONAL MENOPAUSE

1

FACING THE TRUTH

I was lying in bed at 3:00 in the morning, my heart racing, covered in sweat, and all I could think about was, "Oh, damn, not again!" I was consumed by a feeling of despair. I felt this surge of heat that started at the bottom of my feet and slowly flowed through every limb. It continued to flow up my body and straight to the top of my head, causing my heart to start pounding. This surge of heat felt like lava spewing from a volcano, as if I was going to spontaneously combust! There was nowhere to run or hide. I had been consumed by this monster once again. There were times I felt like I was having a heart attack.

Having experienced this for months, I finally made up my mind that it was time to surrender and admit that I was going through menopause. I needed to share this shocking secret with my husband. I had been carrying this heavy load for so long that it became normal for me. I felt like I was silently losing my mind. I finally realized keeping this to myself meant I was shutting everyone out; and even though many people cared about me, I felt terribly alone.

Here I am, living with my best friend and confidant, and I felt too embarrassed to sit down and talk about it. I finally admitted that something had to change. Talking to Jay about my innermost thoughts and feelings was crucial in my healing process.

> Even though many people cared about me, I felt terribly alone.

Here I was, entering my 50s, and I was no longer the predictable person I used to be. My body and my emotions were changing. I felt confused and terrified of the person I was becoming. Like a surprise storm in the night, I did not see it coming. I woke up one morning and there was this strange person looking at me in the mirror. She looked just like me, but something was different. I didn't recognize her. She looked tired and her hair was turning gray. She had fine lines that left shadows around her face. How could this be?

CHAPTER 1

It turns out, I was in menopause. That dark secret nobody wants to talk about. Not only did it hijack my body, but it also corrupted the stability of my mind. I wish someone would have warned me about these frightening changes during this stage of my life that would abruptly take over my body. I was completely unprepared. This was the end of my youth – middle age had been preying on me like a stalker, waiting to capture me and hold me hostage. Deep down, I knew I was physically in menopause, but I was not prepared for the mental anguish that accompanied it. I felt a tremendous amount of sadness and grief, as if the younger, more resilient me had passed away. I was in a state of mourning that lasted for what felt like an eternity. Menopause was my new reality.

Menopause is inevitable in most women's lives. The physical, emotional, and mental effects start in perimenopause, heighten in menopause, and start to lessen in postmenopause. Perimenopause starts in our early 40s, menopause begins in our early 50s, and then postmenopause stays with us for the rest of our lives. This can be a long time to suffer if we don't get help for our symptoms.

So, what is this mysterious monster we call menopause? The technical term for menopause is the cessation of your menstrual cycle for at least 12 months. It is the end of a woman's reproductive years. Many women do not realize there is a transition before menopause called perimenopause. Your estrogen and progesterone levels begin to fluctuate, your periods may become irregular, you may start having mood swings, feel more irritable, experience hot flashes, and notice increased sleep disturbances at night. Less noticeable symptoms may be vaginal dryness, which can lead to discomfort during intercourse. This may cause you to have a decrease in your libido. We then transition into menopause, where we see a more dramatic decline in our estrogen and progesterone levels. Menopause can last for several years, depending on diet and lifestyle factors. We then spend the rest of our lives in postmenopause.

> There is a stigma about menopause: many view it as an end to your vitality.

There is a stigma around the subject of menopause. Perhaps this is why no one wants to talk about it. Our parents were never taught about it so they did not have the foresight to teach us. So here we are, generation after generation, hiding in unnecessary shame and fear of this change in our lives. Every woman goes through this inevitable change. We may have different ideas and perceptions regarding this subject, but we still experience the physical changes in our bodies.

CHAPTER 1

There is a stigma about menopause: many view it as an end to your vitality, which contributes to the culture of silence around menopause.

I used to look forward to entering menopause for many reasons. Most importantly, was the absence of my menstrual cycle. I never wanted to have children, and it was a huge relief knowing that I would no longer have the ability to get pregnant. I also suffered with endometriosis my entire adult life, so this meant no more painful periods each month. No more birth control pills – bonus! I imagined that menopause was a dream come true. Well, it didn't happen that way. It was more like a bad dream that would not end.

Everything started out fine, with an occasional hot flash here and there, but nothing to really concern me. I thought to myself, *I got this. I'm going to do it naturally and without the use of synthetic medications.*

What seemed like overnight, I started having an occasional hot flash at work, then I started getting those warm waves of lava that would pulsate through my body. They were so severe at times I literally thought I would explode. They would come out of nowhere, sending me on a frenzy of disrobing, only to be freezing cold 10 minutes later making me want to grab my sweater again. I'm sure my coworkers thought I was going insane.

Then, it started happening at night. It eventually went from one or two hot flashes to upwards of 30 during the night. I was up and down, tossing and turning all night. I tried to be as quiet as possible so I wouldn't wake my husband. I was working 12-hour shifts as a nurse in a psychiatric hospital, which meant I had to always be on my A-game. Not only was I sleep deprived, but I was also frustrated and completely exhausted. I felt like I was going to have a nervous breakdown.

I also noticed an anger that was building inside of me. I was short-tempered and had little to no patience with those around me. I had sudden bursts of anger and anxiety that would creep into my mind while at work. People would approach me, and I would want to rip off their heads. I would go home and feel embarrassed, anxious, and depressed at how I reacted to others, yet I had no control over these emotions. It was as if I was possessed by the *menopause demon*. I felt that if I didn't get help soon, I would alienate myself from all my family, friends, and coworkers.

Deep down inside, I felt like I was weak. I did not want to talk about what was bothering me for fear of looking like a

CHAPTER 1

weak woman. I know this sounds crazy, but I never wanted to be *one of those people* who constantly complained about their aches and pains. I have always been a strong and independent woman. I come from a long line of strong women, and I was told it was a sign of weakness to ask for help. The men and women were equally tough – working hard – not complaining. Nobody asked for help.

Now don't get me wrong. When one of my uncles needed a new roof, everyone pitched in. No one had to ask for help. Uncles were up on the roof, the kids helped on the ground sending supplies up the ladder, and the women kept them fed and hydrated. It worked like a symphony. Everyone knew what had to be done with one goal in mind... to help a loved one. It was an unspoken rule – family comes first. We all pitched in and did what was needed. When the work was done, everyone was smiling, laughing, and talking about old times.

In my family there was no room for negative thinking or selfishness. If one of us complained about not having those Jordache jeans or those Converse tennis shoes, the look staring back at us was piercing and defeating at the same time. We just knew better. We were told to appreciate what we had. I learned early on that I needed to be strong and to not ask for things selfishly. I knew my parents loved me unconditionally; but attempting to convince them of my desperate need for those Jordache jeans was not appropriate and should not be a priority. Everyone was so busy working and making a living, there was no time for expressing feelings and emotions. I knew my parents worked hard and I did not want to put another burden on them.

Going through the journey of menopause gave me the courage to start talking to my loved ones about my feelings. I had to speak up, not only for my survival, but for the sake of my job and my marriage. Jay and I sat down one evening, and I told him that I needed to talk to him about something important. I was finally able to open up and express how I was feeling emotionally and physically. I began by telling him that I was surrendering – and that I desperately needed help. I could no longer pretend that I was fine and that I had everything under control.

> Going through the journey of menopause gave me the courage to talk to my loved ones about how I was feeling.

This was one of the hardest things I had ever done. Once I started expressing myself, the words started pouring out of me like a flash flood. The look on his face immediately told me he was relieved. He took me in his arms and held

CHAPTER 1

me for what seemed like an eternity. He kissed me and then proceeded to share his feelings with me. He told me that he had been worried about me for months. He went to say he felt like our marriage was in jeopardy at times.

Most days were challenging for him. He was afraid to approach me because he had no idea what kind of mood I would be in when I came home. Was it the fun and loveable Angela, or was it the tired, mean, and frustrated Angela? We sat talking for hours and opened our hearts to each other. We had one of the deepest conversations that we'd had in a long time.

We blocked everything out. Cell phones were turned off – no television on – we even turned off the music that we normally have playing in the background. We began talking about what I was experiencing. I was finally able to express in words how I was feeling physically, mentally, and emotionally. I no longer had those feelings of guilt and shame.

I explained what a hot flash feels like at 2:00 in the morning – like lava flowing inside of me. I told him how I would throw the covers off, attempting to cool my body down. Then I would wake up again, shivering from the dampness that was left behind. I said out loud, "This is a vicious cycle and I feel like I'm in hell." I detailed how I would force myself to get up and go to the bathroom so I could put cold water on my body to cool off. I was exhausted! I wasn't exaggerating when I told Jay that most nights, I woke up 20-30 times a night from those horrible night sweats. My body felt like it was in a burning inferno of hell. I was ready to explode!

Why did I keep the suffering to myself for so long? Why didn't I want to wake up my husband? It was bad enough that I had to experience this exhaustion – I did not want him to have to suffer as well. I feared that if I told him what I was experiencing, he would get up and try to help me in some way. Knowing this, I suffered silently. I did not want to put this burden on him. Remember, I was a strong woman. I felt I could handle this on my own.

Finally having that talk with my husband felt like a weight had been lifted off my shoulders. I quickly realized I did not have to suffer in silence anymore. My husband is my best friend and my confidant. He is the closest person to me, so why wouldn't I share my feelings with him?

We decided that we would brainstorm together. I vowed that I would no longer keep my feelings to myself and that I would allow him to help me in this new stage of my life – our life. For the first time since I started menopause, I

CHAPTER 1

could finally allow myself to talk openly about how I was feeling. We were a team – and I immediately felt empowered. We were a force to be reckoned with!

After a lengthy discussion, Jay put on his thinking cap and said let's start with your doctor. This is a person who has known you and has helped you with your health needs before menopause. This should be the first person we engage to help you navigate through this time of your life.

I called my gynecologist first. During my appointment, I explained to her all the symptoms I was having. I bluntly asked her if I was in full-blown menopause. She light-heartedly told me that since I had not had a menstrual cycle in over a year, I more than likely was in menopause. I asked her if she could run some blood tests to confirm it. She was hesitant at first. She said since I was 51 years old and had not had a menstrual cycle for 12 consecutive months, there was no need to run any tests.

At this point in my life, I was someone who had never desired children, and the prospect of potentially becoming pregnant filled me with fear and anxiety. It was crucial for me to be certain that I had entered menopause, so I insisted on the bloodwork. The gynecologist understood my concern and finally agreed. She suggested that

SOLVING THE MYSTERY OF MENOPAUSE

I consult my primary care physician for the necessary tests. This surprised me because I had initially expected my gynecologist to play a more significant role in guiding me through this transitional phase. While she did present two options – doing nothing or taking prescription medication – neither seemed suitable for me.

At the time, I was bound and determined to go as *natural* as possible. I was not going to take a prescription medication that carried with it risks and side effects that could be detrimental to my health. There was a lot of controversy in the media regarding Hormone Replacement Therapy (HRT) and I felt I needed more education before I just put a pill in my mouth. Don't get me wrong, I am a big believer in taking the right medication for the right reason. As a nurse, I have seen medications significantly help patients get better and even save their lives. But this was something that was going into my body. This was not a life-or-death situation; therefore I felt it was worth exploring alternatives more in depth.

I then made an appointment with my general physician's office. They ran my labs and confirmed what my gynecologist had stated. I was in menopause! I immediately felt relief. I then said to myself, "Now what?" I still needed relief from

CHAPTER 1

these terrible symptoms that had plagued me for over a year. The guessing was finally over and now I had to think about the options that were given to me.

When I went to my appointment with my primary care physician, I asked them if they had any other suggestions other than the ones previously given to me by my gynecologist. She suggested the same two options. She added a suggestion that I take a natural supplement that came from Europe. She stated, "several of my patients have had great success with it." The downside was that it cost $130 a month, not including shipping and handling from abroad. I was ready to do just about anything to feel better, but I wasn't going to go broke. The cost was not feasible for me at the time. There had to be an easier way to find relief.

Feeling defeated, I broke down and tried an over-the-counter supplement suggested by my cousin. I started to see results within the first month. Hot flashes lessened and my sleep improved dramatically. This lasted for about one year, then the hot flashes started increasing and I was experiencing sleepless nights once again. Frustrated, and on the brink of tears, I broke down and told my husband that I was feeling hopeless. I thought to myself, "now what?" We discussed not only my feelings, but also the frustration I experienced from not getting any relief from the night sweats, lack of sleep, and feeling irritable and anxious all the time.

Jay became instrumental in my mental and emotional wellbeing throughout this trying time of my life. He is the calmest and most understanding person I know. He is patient and kind and always knows how to diffuse a difficult situation. We have always been open with each other, but this was a very hard thing to talk about. I did not want to show him any signs of weakness. He loves having a strong woman who knows what she wants and who never complains. We have such a loving relationship, and I did not want to ever say hurtful things to him. I wanted to return to the "happy me." He did not marry an angry and hateful woman; but that's who I felt I was becoming. I felt irritable and angry most of the time. I even found myself being sharp-tongued during many of our conversations. It was very difficult to hear some of the words that came out of my mouth. Once I realized what I had said, I would feel petrified and would immediately apologize. I knew that was a poor excuse, and deep down, I knew I needed help. Something had to change, and it needed to change now!

CHAPTER 1

Jay suggested we look at other treatment options and seek more non-traditional help from other types of physicians. I should mention to you that he's not only my husband, but he is also a pharmacist. He had genuine concern for me, and because of his background in anatomy and physiology, he understands how hormones work in the body. I felt completely confident in what he was suggesting. He went on to explain about working with a type of physician that could spend more time with me, conduct more thorough testing on my hormone levels, and help me find alternative solutions that would put an end to my suffering. I was at my wits' end at this point and willing to try anything.

We did some research together and found a physician that had a strong background as a family medicine practitioner. What resonated with me was that she also specialized in alternative or integrative medical treatments with an emphasis in balancing hormones. Jay pointed out that this type of physician would dive deeper into the foundational issues of what I was experiencing. He went on to explain that traditional medical treatment focuses on alleviating symptoms; but the risk was, we could be missing out on finding the root cause of the illness. Sometimes, that can take a lot of time.

Adding a physician with a focus in integrative medicine would give me that extra edge I needed. They would dedicate more time answering all of my questions, have the resources to run more detailed tests, and help me pinpoint what was causing my symptoms. By creating a team, I no longer felt that I was going through this alone. I had to take responsibility and start on my path to healing. I opened myself up, took a crash course in menopause, and allowed myself to let others in. I did not realize at the time, I was not only becoming an expert in menopause, but I was also becoming an expert in *me*.

> I was not only becoming an expert in menopause, but I was also becoming an expert in me.

CHAPTER 1

THE 3 STAGES OF NATURAL MENOPAUSE	
Perimenopause (On average, this phase lasts 1-3 years)	
Ovaries become less responsive to luteinizing hormone (LH) and follicular stimulating hormone (FSH)	Hormone levels might fluctuate
Mood swings	Estrogen levels drop
Irregular periods	
Menopause	
Decline in estrogen production, which triggers progesterone decline	Menstruation has ceased for 12 or more consecutive months
Menstruation stops	Loss of reproductive function
Ovaries stop releasing an egg each month	
Postmenopause	
After menstruation has ceased for more than 12 consecutive months	FSH levels will continue to rise dramatically as ovaries stop working
Estrogen and progesterone are low and stay pretty stable	May still have menopausal symptoms

From the Institute for Integrative Nutrition-Hormone Health Course, module 20

YOU ARE NOT ALONE

The physical symptoms and changes of menopause that we discussed in Chapter 1 can lead to feelings of isolation. The shame and embarrassment that is often associated with menopause can leave us feeling alone. Most of us are usually unprepared for this new phase in our life. This transition can appear to happen suddenly, catching us off guard.

Menopause usually coincides with other life changes as well. During this time, our children graduate high school, go to college, get married and start their own families. This can lead to the empty nest syndrome that includes additional feelings of grief and loneliness. Gone are the busy days of raising your children while focusing on your career.

Another major change at this time may be the aging of our parents. They were strong and independent at one time, raising us, and then helping us to raise our own children. Often, we do not recognize the signs that our parents are getting older until something dire happens. One of them may fall and break their hip, or they may suddenly get sick and need hospitalization. It is not until then that we realize how fragile they are, and the reality of their immortality occurs to us.

Becoming an empty-nester while having aging parents can have an impact on our emotional wellbeing. The loneliness and feeling of isolation can also put a burden on the relationship we have with our spouse. Now that the children are out of the house, we must re-learn how to live as newlyweds again, just the two of us. For many of us, our life was spent focusing on our children and our marriage was put on the back burner. We may have lost the intimacy we once shared, and we soon realize that we don't know how to have an adult conversation with our spouse. All these changes can be frightening.

CHAPTER 2

Another contributing factor to feeling alone is if we are surrounded by people, particularly at work, who are not at the same stage in life that we are. I felt a sense of embarrassment when I would start to have a hot flash at work. I would go to the air conditioner and attempt to turn the temperature down, although normally we were freezing in our office and anyone who dared turn the air down was given a look of pure evil. I did not want to be ridiculed by my peers, so I kept silent about what was happening to me. Most of my co-workers were 15-20 years younger than me and had no idea what a hot flash felt like. They were young, vibrant, and still bearing children of their own. They did not experience the aches and pains that I was feeling, and certainly did not want to hear about mine. I finally realized that I was ashamed of what I felt I had become – an older woman in menopause. I tried my best to put a smile on my face and pretend that nothing was wrong. I said to myself, *Why would they want to hear about my nagging symptoms of menopause?*

> I thought to myself, *What in the hell has happened to me?*

I felt like my life was deteriorating. I started to focus on my weight gain and the fine wrinkles that were forming on my face. My hair was becoming gray, and it was dry and coarse. I thought to myself, *What in the hell has happened to me?* I used to feel and act young. I didn't have to worry about my skin and hair. Although I was never *skinny*, I was always able to maintain a healthy weight and lose those extra pounds with little to no effort. Now I was self-conscious about how I looked, what I wore, and even what I ate. This, of course, led to eating more comfort foods. I was too exhausted to cook so I ate whatever was easy and convenient – which meant unhealthy. I would also have wine in the evenings in an attempt to help numb all of those unwanted feelings.

These bad habits led to more weight gain and increased feelings of depression. This soon became a vicious cycle. The more I ate bad food and sat on the couch watching movies, the more severe the hot flashes became at night. That turned into more sleepless nights – more irritability – subsequently, brain fogginess the next day. I was on a roller-coaster that would not stop. I felt like I was in the movie "Groundhog Day." My life and my symptoms were on repeat.

> I was on a roller coaster that would not stop.

I soon realized that I was isolating myself from others, including my spouse. I would decline invitations to go out with others because of the shame that I felt about

CHAPTER 2

my appearance. My husband would ask me out on dates in order to cheer me up. I would decline most of the time because I knew I had nothing decent to wear. My clothes no longer fit – they were too tight – and I just didn't like the way I felt. I allowed all these negative thoughts of embarrassment and shame to rule my brain once again. There were times I was even too embarrassed to get undressed in front of my own husband. I was afraid he would look at me and find me unattractive. If I felt that way about myself, how on earth could I go out in public?

When Jay and I finally talked, I asked him how he really felt about the situation. I told him how I was feeling shameful and embarrassed about how I looked. I even asked him how he could still find me attractive. He would always tell me that I was as beautiful as the day he married me, and he loved me no matter what. He would go on to explain that we both had changed during our marriage. He replied, "Why would I desire another woman when I find you attractive?" He told me that I was his best friend, and we would tackle this change together, as husband and wife. He reassured me that he loved me just the way I was and that he had no intention of ever leaving me.

We sat there and held onto each other for what felt like hours. I could tell by the look on his face that he was relieved to finally have this conversation with me. We were finally able to talk about what was going on with me physically and emotionally. After many conversations between the two of us, he was able to express how he was feeling as well. As it turned out, he was also feeling alone and isolated.

When we first met, we only had one rule. We would come home from work and discuss everything that happened during the day, good and bad. This was a way to purge our brain of all the thoughts from the day. We would get it out in the open, work through it, and then move on with our day. It finally dawned on me that we had not sat down and had one of those deep conversations in quite a long time. Now, we had an open line of communication, and we both had our best friend back. He reassured me that we were both aging, but we were doing it together. And doing it with a partner who loves you unconditionally sure makes it less painful. This was one gift of menopause – reconnecting with my husband.

> One gift of menopause was reconnecting with my husband.

CHAPTER 2

The more I was open with others – my husband, friends, and coworkers – the more I realized this was not as taboo a subject as I had once thought. I couldn't believe how willing women were to share their own personal experiences with menopause. Sharing helped us feel less isolated and alone. I encourage you to reach out to family members, friends, and even coworkers. Explore social media pages that have menopause blogs; or attend support groups in your local area or online. I also found a lot of useful information listening to podcasts on my way to work each morning.

The more you talk about what you are experiencing, the less isolated you will feel. There is actually a plethora of knowledge at your fingertips. I also decided to join an online support group. I found many like-minded women who felt just as alone and afraid as I did. I learned coping skills, found online resources to help with my hot flashes, and I was able to create new friendships with many of the women in the group. I had allowed these feelings and bad habits to plague me for almost two years. It was such a relief when I connected with others and realized that I was *not* alone.

I still have occasional days where I allow those old feelings of shame and self-doubt creep in, but I no longer hold onto these negative feelings. After more self-reflection, I realized that I was focusing on the past, and the negative feelings that accompanied it. I felt like I was spiraling out of control, and I was desperate for a change – a change in my mindset and a change in my health. In order for this to happen, I needed to let go of the past and not allow my present feelings to take over. I am now able to recognize these old patterns, and I use them as fuel to motivate myself to be the strong and confident woman that I am.

The online support group really empowered me to take control over my negative thoughts. I learned coping skills, found online resources to help with my hot flashes, and I was able to make new friendships with many of the women in the group. For the first time since I began this journey of menopause, I felt prepared for this new stage of my life.

> You are your own best doctor – you should earn a PhD in you.

I encourage you to take that first step to help yourself. You'll find that you are not alone in this journey. This book will help you, or your loved one, navigate the endless signs, symptoms and feelings associated with menopause. I encourage you to explore some of the suggestions this book provides for you and do your own research. You are your own best doctor – you should earn a PhD in *you*. Nobody knows exactly what you are thinking or feeling. Each person has their own unique signs and symptoms of menopause.

A good example is when a patient is given the diagnosis of cardiovascular disease. Some patients may have had a heart attack or stroke, others have blocked arteries. The treatment is different and unique to each person. Menopause should be the same. We deserve to have personalized treatment for our individualized symptoms.

So, where do you start finding information? This is probably the hardest part. I searched numerous websites for anything that would help me. There is a lot of information out there. But is it valid information? And does it apply to me? I found hundreds of solutions, but for every solution I also found what appears to be a valid contradiction. I was confused and frustrated. I am a nurse and I know the science behind menopause, but even I felt lost. Dr. Google can be a great source of information for users, as it provides a plethora of information, but it can also be dangerous. There is a lot of misleading information out there. This can lead to false hopes and cause unnecessary fears.

I read countless articles, listened to hundreds of podcasts, and I even purchased a dozen or so books on the subject. After all of this, I realized that the same information was repeated and given in all these different avenues. They all provided *cookie-cutter* answers such as: hot flashes, night sweats, anxiety, depression, brain fog, weight gain, inflammation, and fatigue. They would give suggestions of hormone replacement therapy, the use of bio-identical hormones, nutritional guidelines, and a long list of medical jargon about the numerous hormones in our bodies.

As a healthcare professional, I found this multitude of information was even more confusing. I became more depressed and anxious because I was not finding the answers that I was looking for. I felt that I wasted countless hours searching for what appeared to be repeated information. My husband scoured through numerous medical journals only to come to the same conclusion as I had. Despite his extensive knowledge as a pharmacist, assisting me through menopause had proven to be a challenge due to the complexities of emotional, physical, and hormonal factors that plagued me. Together, we concluded that we would need to do even more research and experiment with different modalities in order to assist me in finding relief from my symptoms.

LET'S TALK ABOUT IT

Let's dive deeper into how important it is to have more in-depth conversations with your spouse, partner, friends and even your children. Breaking the silence may feel like it is the hardest part; but once you break down those barriers, open your heart, and share your feelings, you will feel a deep sense of relief. Sharing them is a way to take control over your feelings and emotions. Once you acknowledge them, it enables you to understand yourself better, make informed decisions, and cultivate a healthier and more fulfilling life.

The easiest place to start is with your female friends and acquaintances. You will find that many of them are also going through similar circumstances. Start by asking the simple question, "What is your first thought when you hear the word menopause?" You will be surprised by the similar answers you will hear. Most women will mention the hot flashes, mood swings and weight gain. Menopause can be all those things, and so much more. The more you talk about your experience with menopause the easier it will be to continue these conversations with others. You will realize that you are not alone in this journey. Sharing stories and solutions with others can benefit you tremendously.

> You are not alone in this journey.

A few years ago, a friend of mine threw a party for all her pre- and postmenopausal friends. We were instructed to bring any leftover condoms, birth control aids, and all leftover feminine hygiene products with us to the party. We enjoyed a nice dinner with some amazing wine and talked about our lives. We spent the evening laughing, crying, and even getting angry at times while talking about our on-going battle with our menopausal symptoms.

CHAPTER 3

We then continued our party outside and proceeded to build a bonfire in the backyard. We even brought sticks and marshmallows, reminding us of our past and the carefree moments of childhood. We then placed all our feminine hygiene products into the fire, one by one, while exclaiming our freedom from the constraints of the past. We gloriously danced around the fire – laughing, holding hands, and sharing our most intimate thoughts at that moment.

I finally felt empowered and free from the chains of this thing called menopause. The emotional bonds that were formed that night left a permanent imprint in my heart and my mind. It was amazing to purge all those unwanted, negative feelings. It was also a beneficial way to bond with other women who were also going through the same experiences. This can be a time to laugh, cry, get mad, and even make fun of what may seem like an embarrassing situation.

> I finally felt empowered and free from the chains of this thing called menopause.

If you do not have any close, personal friends to talk to, there are many other ways to reach out and connect with women experiencing the same issues. Social media can be a great tool. I use Facebook groups for helpful information and to connect with others. Hearing others' stories helps to validate your own thoughts and feelings. It is also a great way to meet people and build new friendships. There are a lot of groups out there. Some contain negative talk, so go online and join several to see what information they have and view the comments. Join and interact with the groups that resonate with you and that have the most useful information for your situation.

Instagram also has support groups as well as a multitude of funny jokes and anecdotes about how other women are coping with menopause. While I try to limit my social media time, I do find that watching Instagram feeds regarding menopause can instantaneously turn my day around from feeling sad and depressed to feeling happy and laughing hysterically. Tik Tok, Twitter, and YouTube also have helpful information, and can be a great way to find humor in your situation. One benefit of menopause is that you can enjoy having multiple personalities each day. I can go from feeling hot, angry, and crying one moment to laughing and smiling in an instant. No wonder women want to keep this secret hidden in the closet!

There are many risks to not talking with your loved ones, your physician, or just not admitting to yourself how you

CHAPTER 3

are feeling. When you shut down and do not talk about this sensitive subject, you can feel isolated and alone. My husband expressed that he felt alone and that there was a wedge coming between us. He felt like I was drifting away from him and our marriage. I was unknowingly shutting him out mentally and physically. I would pull away from intimacy because I felt tired, irritable, and just plain fat! I didn't want to look at myself without clothes and felt my husband would not want to look at me either. I was fearful that he would feel turned off by my weight gain. My clothes were tight and simply just didn't fit me anymore. I had excess belly fat, enlarged breasts, and my face looked round and puffy. I had this horrible nightmare playing in my head that kept telling me I was ugly, fat, and disgusting. How terrible is that? I allowed my thoughts to take me into those deep, dark places where no one should go.

By talking about how I was feeling, he showed me unconditional love and compassion for what I was going through. We now feel a deeper connection with each other. I feel safe talking about anything and everything with him now. I no longer feel the shame or embarrassment of menopause that crippled me for months. This has brought us closer than we have ever been to each other.

SOLVING THE MYSTERY OF MENOPAUSE

A lot of men are taught to keep their feelings inside and not share how they feel. If you have a male partner, tell him that you need him and truly want him to help you during this time. Emphasize that you want to be closer to him both emotionally and physically.

Men really do want to help you, but they may have a hard time understanding those *silent clues.* Don't expect them to understand every hint you give them. You must map it out with your man. Guys love reading maps and they love lists. They will read instructions, so give them a list of things that you wish they would do to help you feel better. Together you can map out a plan to help you emotionally and possibly even strengthen your marriage.

If he insists on shutting you out, reach out to other women and ask how they talked to their male partners. They might have suggestions on how you can encourage your spouse to open up and talk about things. You could even ask to talk to your friends' spouses to get a man's perspective on the subject. If your spouse insists on not talking about it, don't force the subject as you can make things worse between the two of you. Find an outlet with other sources to find the emotional support that you need.

CHAPTER 3

Seeking the help of a professional therapist is beneficial in many ways. It provides a safe and non-judgmental space for individuals to express their thoughts and feelings. Therapists can help you identify and modify negative behavior patterns, improve communication skills, and help you navigate relationships more effectively. They can also provide tools and techniques to help you regulate your emotions and manage symptoms so that you can navigate future challenges more effectively.

Menopause has many ugly faces. It shows up in each person in its own unique way. I have talked to many women who state that they have had no physical or emotional symptoms of menopause, while others have suffered tremendously. There are women that may benefit from the help of prescription medications to help with increased anxiety or depression. Others may find relief in meditation and self-reflection. No matter which route you choose, know that it is OK to ask for help. You do not have to suffer in silence.

For those of you that have children, I urge you to talk to them about menopause. My mother never had this conversation with me, which meant I did not understand what was happening with her. The only thing she said about menopause was that she had terrible hot flashes. She was angry and irritable all the time. This put a heavy strain on our relationship for many years. She would get angry with me, and we would go days without speaking to each other. There were even times when I told her that she needed to apologize to me for the way she was treating me. She finally realized how her mood was placing a wedge between us so she chose to go on hormone replacement therapy. I finally got my mom back, and we now have an open and loving relationship. We now look back and can laugh and joke about those dark times.

Finally, you want to have open lines of communication with your physician. What is your relationship with your physician like? Are you able to have these open conversations? Have you ever left the office, got in your car, and hit your hand on the steering wheel thinking, *Why did I forget to ask about this?* Unfortunately, most physicians only have 15 minutes to spend with their patients. Medicaid and Medicare dictate how many patients a physician must see in a day and this drastically limits the amount of quality time they are able to spend with you.

Here are a few tips on how to be a better patient for your doctor:

CHAPTER 3

1. Be clear and concise about the purpose of the appointment.
2. Write your questions down ahead of time so you are prepared.
3. Take someone to the appointment with you to keep you on track and take notes on the doctor's suggestions.
4. Be completely transparent about what you are feeling both physically and emotionally. If you are not completely honest with your physician, they will have a hard time helping you.

These simple steps will help you get the most out of the time you spend with your physician. When you come to your appointment prepared, your doctor can spend his or her time helping you find solutions, instead of trying to guess what is wrong with you. This is helpful for all situations, not just menopause. For example, if you omit how much fast food you eat, your lack of exercise or the two glasses of wine that you drink every evening, your doctor will not have the whole picture of what is going on with you. This can stop you from finding the answers that you need.

Your doctor can be an amazing resource for you. He or she may not be able to help you in every area that you need, but can refer you to someone who can. If you feel that you do not have an open relationship with your primary care physician, then I encourage you to reach out to your gynecologist or your alternative or integrative medicine doctor. You also have the choice to get a second opinion from another physician if you are not happy with the one that you have. Many primary care physicians are great at treating medical issues such as diabetes or hypertension, but they may not have a lot of experience in women's health issues.

This is where a specialist comes in. I was not satisfied with the suggestions my primary care doctor, or my gynecologist gave me, so I reached out to a physician that specializes in integrative medicine. She spent an entire hour with me, asking me in-depth questions and truly getting to know me. For the first time, I felt like I was being heard. Integrative medical doctors attempt to find the root cause of your issue so that they can find optimal solutions. They are not looking at and treating you solely based on your symptoms. They treat the underlying condition with traditional medicine and incorporate natural therapies as well.

My doctor did extensive lab work that included blood work, urine, and saliva samples. I received a detailed report of what hormones and vitamin and mineral deficiencies that I had. My second visit was almost an hour as well. She went into detail about all my lab results and offered suggestions of how we could improve the deficiencies found in my lab work. This was the first time since I started my journey with menopause that I truly felt a sense of hope. I finally found a doctor who truly understood what I was going through and helped me find solutions.

Integrative medical practitioners not only provide education to their patients, but also empower them to actively manage their well-being. They dedicate significant time to each patient, adopting a holistic approach that addresses the individual as a whole, rather than merely treating symptoms. Personally, I've opted for bioidentical hormone therapy. This requires a biannual physical examination that ensures my hormonal balance is accurately maintained.

> Integrative medical practitioners empower patients to actively manage their well-being.

One thing to note, most insurance companies usually will not pay for services performed outside of standard medical care. I had to pay out of pocket for my office visit and my lab work, but it has been worth every dollar. It is a feeling of freedom knowing that I have a choice in my healthcare.

I am truly satisfied with my doctor and my results so far. My only regret is that I did not make this choice earlier. I spent two long and miserable years suffering in silence. My hope in writing this book is to help you find the right people, tools, and resources so that you do not go through the same things that I went through. This book is meant to empower every woman to take charge of their physical and emotional wellbeing, once and for all.

If your partner is having a hard time understanding what you are going through, here are a few suggestions that can help open the lines of communication between the two of you. Ask your partner to:

- Listen and be supportive.
- Understand that some (not all) mood changes may be due to menopause.
- Allow you to express your feelings, even if they aren't understood.
- Help you understand the symptoms.
- Allow you to talk about what you need and when you need it.

There are many websites that contain helpful information for men and how they can better understand menopause and what you are going through. If you feel that you are

CHAPTER 3

not able to communicate effectively with your partner, counseling is another great option. Some of the benefits are improved communication, conflict resolution, identifying negative patterns, preventing future issues, and improved intimacy between the two of you.

Men and women have different communication styles, which makes having these conversations difficult and even frustrating at times. Having an outlet to speak about your feelings can be crucial in repairing and maintaining your close and personal relationships. For those of you who do not have a supportive partner in your life, I encourage you to reach out to friends or family. You can build a supportive community of friends from Facebook groups and menopause blogs. In these groups you can find a circle of women who, like yourself, are facing similar struggles and challenges. Support groups are also an incredible way to share your story in a safe, non-threatening environment. Listening to others can give you a sense of hope, reminding you that you are not alone. This is a time to share similar experiences with women who have a mutual understanding of your journey.

> *Surround yourself with only people*
> *who are going to lift you higher.*
> **—OPRAH WINFREY**

LET'S HAVE SOME FUN

Eventually I learned how to have some fun with this stage of life. Thank goodness I did because it really helped. Once we reach menopause, we are already familiar with experiencing physical and emotional changes caused by our hormones. We go through puberty and the start of a menstrual cycle. Many of us also experience side effects such as menstrual cramping, bloating, mood swings, and acne breakouts (which I had well into my 40s). We then enter adulthood where many women suffer from uterine fibroids, cysts, and even endometriosis. Next, we find that perfect mate, get married and start a family. Now we have to figure out the hormonal changes of pregnancy. Just when we think we have it all figured out, we start having perimenopausal symptoms in our 40s and then menopause in our 50s.

You might be saying to yourself, *Something's gotta give.* How is it that we are still able to work, raise a family, and keep a smile on our face when we have gone through so much in our lives? *This is a testament to the resilience of women!*

For many years I had looked forward to menopause as a time when the pain of endometriosis would end. I used to declare loudly, "I can't wait for menopause, so I don't have to deal with the pain of endometriosis." There would also be no more cramping and pain every month. I would not have to worry about feminine hygiene products or be afraid to wear white anymore. My adult acne would disappear... so, it was a shock when menopause came and I had a whole new set of unpleasant symptoms.

Once I saw the doctor of integrated medicine and managed my symptoms with hormone therapy, there were many positives to menopause. There was no more fear of having an accidental pregnancy. For my entire menstruating life this fear lingered in the back of my mind. Finding myself in menopause was a dream because it meant not having to

CHAPTER 4

go to the pharmacy for birth control pills, no more using uncomfortable condoms, and no more interference from my menstrual cycle. When it was confirmed that I was no longer fertile with a hormone test, it was life changing for me. Having this heavy burden lifted from my mind helped me to fully embrace my newfound freedom, and I was finally able to start having fun with my sexuality. Of course, my husband was ecstatic with the new, more playful me. We could now make love anytime we wanted without the constraints of my hormonal past.

> We could now make love anytime we wanted without the constraints of my hormonal past.

I looked forward to taking more vacations since I no longer had to plan them around my menstrual cycle. For years, I felt a constant worry when planning our trips. I had to pack enough pain medication, such as Aleve and Tylenol, to help alleviate the inevitable pain I would experience. I also had to pack something to counteract the heartburn from using those pain medicines. There were times that I got fed up and just said *no* to traveling if I was going to be on my period. Low libido had taken a toll on my marriage. You can imagine how excited I was when I finally ceased to have a menstrual cycle. It was one of the most glorious things I experienced during this journey. I was finally getting my groove back.

Having a low libido may not always be physical, it can also stem from a lack of emotional intimacy. We unknowingly pull ourselves away from our partners due to the increased stress, weight gain, vaginal dryness, and low energy that accompanies menopause. I had to teach myself how to express my wants and desires to my husband. When I had a stressful day and asked him for touch, he lovingly responded to me. When I started paying attention to my body and my emotions, I realized that my decrease in libido came from my own automatic negative thoughts (ANTS). These are spontaneous, involuntary, and often subconscious thoughts that are characterized by negativity and pessimism. Habitual, negative self-talk can train the brain to see things pessimistically. When left unchecked, negative thinking can distort perceptions of reality. Negative thinking can effectively rewrite your brain's neural networks, reinforcing pathways that make it more likely you'll continue seeing the glass as half empty. For more information visit: *www.brainmd.com*.

The average human has approximately 70,000 thoughts per day (*www.healthybrains.org*). You can imagine the

CHAPTER 4

potential damage we are doing to ourselves when we do not control these negative thoughts. Each time you have a negative thought, tell yourself to *STOP*, and replace it with a positive thought. There are many websites and books on the subject of positive thinking. I highly recommend following Louise L. Hay. She has numerous books, audios, videos, and even card decks to help you get started. I have been reading her books for over 30 years. She is a tremendous inspiration.

Now, let's talk about some of the benefits that menopause can have on sexuality. Most of you might read this and think that this concept is unheard of. Well, I for one am here to tell you that it is not. Once I got over the shame of being menopausal, my inner cougar started to come out. I finally embraced this rite of passage and surrendered to this inevitable change. With the help of my husband, I was able to finally enjoy my sexuality once again. I no longer felt embarrassed when I walked around the house naked. I even started wearing my sexy lingerie again. My husband was still turned on by me, which reignited the self-confidence that radiated within me.

There were times when I was having a hot flash that I would take off all my clothes and peek around the corner at my unassuming husband and say, "I'm hot. You don't mind if I walk around naked, do you?" The look on his face was priceless. He would jump up and start chasing me into the bedroom while attempting to disrobe himself. I cannot count the number of times he tripped or ran into the wall trying to take his clothes off. We would jump into the bed, laughing so hard that tears ran down our faces.

> "I'm hot. You don't mind if I walk around naked, do you?"

Most textbooks warn women about losing their libido and experiencing vaginal dryness. For those who suffer from dryness, there are many natural lubricants on the market that can help alleviate the symptoms. This is a time to be spontaneous with your partner. If you need to use over the counter lubricants, try a flavored one. There are even products on the market that give you a tingling sensation. This is a great way to spice things up with your partner. Try experimenting with new positions and different types of lubricants so that intercourse can be comfortable and enjoyable. Sex should be fun and pleasurable for both of you.

Another great way to increase moisture naturally is spending more time enjoying foreplay with your partner rather than focusing on intercourse. Foreplay can allow both of

CHAPTER 4

you to relax and enjoy being in the moment. This simple act of touching and kissing each other can allow your body to lubricate itself naturally. Touch also helps you to unwind and facilitates relaxation of your mind and body by increasing feel-good hormones such as serotonin and dopamine – while decreasing the stress hormones cortisol and epinephrine. If you don't have a partner, you can always book a massage. Laying on a warm table with soft lighting, soft music playing in the background, and essential oils wafting throughout the room will leave you feeling like a wet piece of spaghetti when your session is over. Talk about total relaxation!

I personally crave touch. It can be as simple as my husband rubbing my feet or massaging my head. He knows that when he offers non-sexual touch, I will immediately run to the bedroom, take off all my clothes, and lay in bed with anticipation. It is such a surreal experience for me. I reciprocate the touch and we often end up having an intimate sexual encounter that was entirely spontaneous. Making intimacy a priority has given our relationship a sense of security, trust, and understanding.

Intimacy with Jay was not always about sexual intercourse. We were intimate in many other ways as well. At times, when I was having a hot flash, he would get a cool rag and lovingly wipe the sweat off my body. He would then proceed to touch me softly and kiss me all over my body. I would get goosebumps all over and would be cooled off immediately. When I was having severe hot flashes, he would jump into the shower with me to help cool me down. Having someone you love help wash your body or even assist you to wash your hair can be a very intimate moment.

Even though most of my hot flashes have gone, I still experience them occasionally. Jay continues to take care of me when I am having my menopausal moments. I'm sure he secretly hopes that I will take all my clothes off so he can chase me into the bedroom! We can now laugh and joke about all those nightmarish moments that we shared together. I look forward to this new chapter of my life and the limitless possibilities that lie ahead. This entire experience had brought us closer than we ever could have imagined.

Not many couples share intimate moments together later in their marriage. People get so busy with everyday life that they forget about the simple things. Turning the air conditioner down or getting a fan may not seem important, but when you are going through these changes, all those little things mean a lot. The fact that my husband was paying attention to my mood meant the world to me. He knew exactly what to do to make me feel better.

Think spontaneously and have an intimate weekend together. Book a cabin in the middle of nowhere and make sure it has a hot tub. Tell him you accidentally forgot to pack your swimsuit so you have to jump into the water naked. You can always blame it on your menopausal symptoms – I'm sure he won't mind. Pack some sexy lingerie, a bottle of your favorite wine, and bring foods that will enhance your sexual pleasure. Feeding your partner chocolate covered strawberries will make him melt in your arms. Or better yet, cover his chest in chocolate syrup and eat the strawberries off him. This will ignite his sexual prowess.

Surprise your spouse and book a reservation at one of your favorite restaurants. Tell him to put on a nice outfit because you are taking him on a date. Tell him you want to pretend that it's your first date. Hold hands at the dinner table, while flirting and giggling with each other. Gaze into each other's eyes and share your fondest memories of your relationship together. Then, lean over and kiss him gently on the cheek and tell him how much you love and appreciate him. After a night like this, he will want to go on dates more often.

When both of you prioritize self-care as a team, it can lead to great outcomes. You may have gained a few extra pounds during menopause, but that doesn't mean you have to keep the weight on. Ask your partner to help you in the kitchen. Making healthy meals together not only nourishes your body but also strengthens your relationship. You are fostering a shared commitment to build a foundation for a healthier, happier life. Couples who cook together also tend to experience delightful and intimate moments that can strengthen their bond. The added benefits of losing weight, increasing your energy, and finding new ways to laugh are worth it. When we were first together, Jay and I would turn on the music and dance together in the middle of the kitchen floor while cooking. Over time, those moments gradually came to a halt. Now is the time to reignite that spark, get healthy, and make cooking fun again!

After you have prepared and eaten your dinner, go for a relaxing walk. Hold hands and enjoy the beauty of nature. This is not only a way to get healthy, but also a great opportunity to open up and share your feelings with each other. Talk about your relationship and share your hopes and

CHAPTER 4

dreams for the future. Be silly and take selfies together, making new memories that will be enjoyed for a lifetime. This is an excellent way to get healthy physically and mentally, while bringing you closer together emotionally.

Even though menopause may have taken control over your life, now is the time to take charge and start living again. Life is meant to be full of joy and laughter. Incorporating self-care into your daily routine can be an effective way to reduce stress and anxiety, increase your self-confidence, and improve your overall mood. When you are happy on the inside, it starts to show on the outside. You begin eating healthier, exercising more, and wanting to engage in more pleasurable activities that brighten your mood. You start to crave those feelings of happiness and euphoria and find yourself surrounded by only positive people and circumstances. You have turned that vicious cycle of defeat into a cycle of hope and possibilities.

THE MENOPAUSE DIARIES

FLYING DOWN THE HIGHWAY, NAKED

Menopause can be a fun and funny time of life. Here is a story of one of those times from Hope, Age 45.

My husband and I wanted to see the Grand Canyon in Arizona. We lived in Nevada and our children were away at college, so we decided to take our time and do the 5-hour drive. I was in perimenopause and having hot flashes all the time. During our drive, I had a hot flash that would not go away. We were in the middle of the desert, it was 110 degrees outside, and I was miserable. I decided to turn the air on full blast and take my clothes off to try and cool down. Well, next thing I knew there were police sirens behind us, and we had to pull over. I was hurrying to put my clothes back on before the deputy got to the car. My husband tried to explain the situation as best as he could as I was feverishly putting my pants back on. It turns out that during my strip tease in the car, my husband lost track of his driving and was going 90 mph. The officer had a chuckle and told us to be safe and let us on our way with no ticket. Talk about an embarrassing situation!

PART 2
PHYSICAL MENOPAUSE

5

A ROLLER COASTER RIDE OF HORMONES

I was fortunate to have grown up in a small town that had an amusement park practically in my backyard. I had a season pass each summer and spent endless hours venturing around the park with my friends. We would run from coaster to coaster, laughing endlessly in sheer delight. I remember the roller coaster and the anticipation of knowing what lay ahead. The ups and downs and the twists and turns evoked a nervous excitement within me. I even let out a few screams along the way. My emotions were just as volatile as the ride – ranging from anticipation and excitement to feeling scared to death. The ride eventually would end, and my emotions went back to feeling relieved that I survived.

> I've discovered a new ride that has more unexpected twists and turns than I ever imagined.

Fast forward 30 years and here I am, riding that roller coaster once again. But this time, I'm not at the amusement park. I've discovered a new ride that has more unexpected twists and turns than I ever imagined. This time I'm exploring the wild journey of hormonal fluctuations and how they can disrupt your life.

So, what are hormones? Hormones are chemical messengers that are produced by your endocrine system. They affect almost every system in your body. They help or regulate metabolism, digestion, blood pressure, your sleep and even your mood, just to name a few. Female sex hormones, or sex steroids, play vital roles in sexual development, reproduction, and general health. Sex hormone levels change over time, but some of the most significant changes happen during puberty, pregnancy, and menopause (*www.medicalnewstoday.com*).

There are three main female hormones that help the body function: estrogen, progesterone, and testosterone.

CHAPTER 5

Estrogen is a group of hormones composed of estradiol, estrone, and estriol. They are produced by the ovaries, adrenal glands, and fat cells and they control many of the female hormonal functions including menstruation, pregnancy, menopause, bone density – and can affect your mood. Estrogen also plays a role in maintaining the moisture of your vaginal wall, collagen production and the moisture of your skin, and can help your ability to focus. During perimenopause and menopause, estrogen levels tend to decline, which can lead to the well-known menopausal symptoms we have discussed.

Estrogen is also needed to make serotonin function properly. Serotonin is one of the body's *feel-good hormones*. Without estrogen, we may feel anxious and depressed. It can also affect critical thinking and short-term memory skills (Dr. Daniel G. Amen: *www.amenclinics.com*).

Progesterone is produced by the ovaries after ovulation. This hormone helps maintain pregnancy and prepare the uterus for fertilization. It also helps regulate your menstrual cycle. Progesterone is also one of the *feel good hormones*. Some scientists call it nature's valium. It helps with sleep, libido, your mood and has an overall calming effect on the mind (*www.hardingmedicalinstitute.com*).

Progesterone is higher in women who are pregnant. That's why many women experience a *high* during pregnancy. Progesterone receptors are highly concentrated in the brain. They support gamma-aminobutyric acid (GABA), a neurotransmitter that calms and relaxes the brain (Dr. Daniel G. Amen: *www.amenclinics.com*).

Levels of estrogen and progesterone start fluctuating in a woman's late 30s to early 40s, which can make us feel irritable and anxious. When levels start to decline during menopause, we may experience irregular periods and mood swings. It is important to know that the symptoms of menopause can be similar to psychiatric conditions such as depression, anxiety and panic attacks. Many women are often misdiagnosed with these rather than fluctuating hormone levels. It is important to have your hormones checked as early as your 30s to get a baseline. Many are in perimenopause without knowing and suffer needlessly.

*See chart for symptoms of high and low estrogen.

> The symptoms of menopause can be similar to psychiatric conditions.

CHAPTER 5

Low Estrogen	High Estrogen
Weight gain	Puffiness
Bladder Incontinence/Infection	Heavy Bleeding
Mood changes/Depression	Fibrocystic Breasts
Insomnia	Low Libido
Low Libido	Cravings for carbs
Heart Palpitations	Weight gain around hips
Osteoporosis	Vaginal/oral yeast (thrush)
Painful Intercourse	Mood swings/quick to cry
Foggy-headedness	Tender Breasts
Irritability	Headaches/migraines
Fatigue	
Weepiness	
Hot Flashes	
Pain	

(Dr. Daniel G. Amen, *Unleash the Power of the Female Brain*, pg 95)

Testosterone, primarily a male hormone, is also found in small amounts in the female body. It is an important regulator of fertility, sexual desire, and bone strength (*www.haneygyn.com*). If your testosterone levels are normal, they help in the retention of muscle mass, bone density, and play a role in your libido, your energy levels and your mood. Testosterone starts to decline in your 30s. Low levels can make you feel tired, experience vaginal dryness, dry skin and nails, thinning hair, and you may lose muscle mass. The largest cause of low testosterone is menopause.

Two other hormones that are markers for menopause are follicle stimulating hormone (FSH) and luteinizing hormone (LH). FSH stimulates your ovaries to produce eggs and estrogen and LH stimulates ovulation. These levels start to rise as your estrogen and progesterone start to decline during your menopausal transition. When a woman's FSH blood level is consistently elevated to 30 mIU/mL or higher, and she has not had a menstrual period for a year, it is generally accepted that she has reached menopause. The raised FSH and low estrogen levels appear to cause the characteristic hot flashes that many women experience.

There are numerous other hormones in the body and various conditions that can arise from a disruption in any or all of these hormones. Working in healthcare and having studied these hormones, I found that all the books and articles that I read were too confusing, even for me. My hope in this book is to bring a general awareness to some of the key topics that are associated with menopause.

During my journey, I have had to make subtle changes to my daily regimen. As my body changes, so do my hormones, vitamin, and mineral levels. I see my physician

CHAPTER 5

every 6 months. She sits with me and listens intently to all my concerns. We work together as a team, both sharing information and discussing recommendations for my overall health. My blood is drawn to check my hormone levels every 6 months as well.

My last visit was a little different. I was feeling more stress and anxiety than usual. I was having trouble sleeping, waking up at 3 am and not being able to go back to sleep. I could not figure out what was happening. During our discussion, she asked important questions and I finally realized where all the stress was coming from. I was writing this book. I have never written a book before. I was still working, and I had just had shoulder surgery. Trying to do my daily chores at home, work and write a book with one good arm was definitely a challenge. I then fractured my ankle, which almost sent me spiraling off the deep end.

My doctor theorized that I may be in adrenal fatigue. Some physicians deny there is such a thing. (This is why it is important to do your own homework and make decisions that you think are best for you.) I agreed with her approach, and together we came up with a game plan. My testosterone levels were a bit high, so we adjusted my bioidentical hormones, and my dehydroepiandrosterone (DHEA) levels were low, so we began supplementing that as well. Within 2 weeks with this new medication change, I started to feel like myself again.

So, what is adrenal fatigue? Although it isn't accepted as a medical diagnosis, it is considered a condition caused by long-term exposure to stressful situations. A person may experience a collection of nonspecific symptoms, such as body aches, fatigue, nervousness, sleep disturbances and digestive problems. Your adrenals are glands that sit on top of your kidneys. They are responsible for the production of adrenaline, DHEA, and cortisol. These hormones are responsible for your fight or flight mode, which is your body's reaction to danger and was designed to help you survive stressful and life-threatening situations. Some of the physical symptoms are dilated pupils, pale or flushed skin, an increase in your heart rate and blood pressure, and even trembling. When you are in a constant state of stress, anxiety, or fear, you wear out your adrenal glands. Here are some of the symptoms of adrenal fatigue: low libido, decreased energy, poor sleep, mental fog, abdominal fat, and depression.

When you are feeling tired, depressed, or you just don't feel like yourself, pay attention. These are signals that

CHAPTER 5

something is going on physically and mentally with your body. Do not wait like I did. Go to your doctor and tell them how you feel. It doesn't matter if they believe in this diagnosis or that supplement, the point is to get help before your symptoms are out of control.

Now that you have a basic understanding of menopause and the hormones that are associated with it, how are you going to take care of yourself and help alleviate some of the symptoms that you may be experiencing? It may be easy to recognize the physical symptoms or a hormone imbalance, but what about the emotional effects? These are much harder to recognize.

Communication is key here. Talk to your spouse, family, and coworkers. Ask them if they have noticed any changes in your overall mood or your behavior. Tell them that you are giving them permission to tell you the truth. They will feel relieved, knowing that they are able to help you without any backlash or grudges held against them.

We all know someone that is angry and in a bad mood most of the time. We can feel the tension and negative energy surrounding them. Everyone tries to avoid them, knowing they may get pulled into their negativity. Yet, nobody stands up and tells this person that they are being rude, hateful, and even a witch. Why do we allow ourselves to be surrounded by this day after day? I feel that most people want to be happy and go about their day without complications. This is why it is important to have open lines of communication with those around you. You don't want to be *that person*.

Sit down and have that deep conversation with your spouse or partner. Effective communication is crucial for strengthening emotional bonds and building a foundation of trust that will allow a healthy and thriving relationship. Initiate the conversation by sharing your thoughts and feelings, both mentally and physically. Just as you have the right to be heard and understood, they also have the right to be informed about your experiences. To ensure effective communication, it should be a two-way street. Encourage your spouse to proactively inquire about your thoughts and experiences during this phase of your life. Keep the lines of communication open, maintaining an atmosphere of non-judgmental understanding. Through this, you both will come to realize that you are a team, capable of navigating this transition together. There are numerous online resources that explain the menopausal process – suggest exploring some of these sites to enhance their understanding.

CHAPTER 5

It is also important for self-reflection. During this phase of your life, your body is telling you it is time to slow down. In a way, it is forcing you to slow down. Take time to reflect regularly on who you are and who you are becoming. Focus on your thoughts and desires, and pay attention to how you are feeling on an emotional level. Many females have a nurturing quality about them. We raise our children, make sure our partner is taken care of, and even watch over our pets. We want to nurture and love unconditionally. The one thing we forget to do is take care of ourselves. We give so much of ourselves to others, we often neglect the most important person – ourselves!

> Take time to reflect regularly on who you are and who you are becoming.

When we ignore our own inner thoughts and desires, we tend to get stuck in a spiral. We do the same things repeatedly, knowing that it makes us unhappy. We never give ourselves the time to really think about what we want, and what we want to change in our lives. Here are some benefits of self-reflection: increased self-awareness, a greater sense of control, improved communication skills, a deeper alignment with your core values, better decision-making skills, and greater accountability (*www.verywellmind.com*).

Taking care of yourself emotionally is important, but what about physically? You have gone to your physician and the two of you have worked out a plan to help alleviate some of those nasty, unwanted physical symptoms. But is it enough? For most of us, it probably is not. We need to be accountable for our own health. We cannot rely on our doctor to fix us. This must be a team effort. We must make better choices in how we treat our bodies.

Prioritizing physical self-care during menopause becomes crucial for women as they navigate through this significant life transition. The hormonal changes accompanying menopause can bring about a range of physical challenges, such as bone density loss, muscle mass decline, and weight fluctuations. Engaging in regular exercise such as walking is crucial for maintaining bone health, managing weight, and alleviating mood swings. Additionally, walking serves as a natural stress reliever, aiding in mood stabilization and combating feelings of anxiety or depression commonly experienced during menopause.

> Sleep is vital for the regulation of hormones, including those that influence mood and stress.

Sleep plays a pivotal role in the well-being of women during menopause, making it an essential component of

CHAPTER 5

overall health and quality of life. Hormonal fluctuations, particularly a decline in estrogen levels, can contribute to symptoms such as hot flashes, night sweats, and mood swings, all of which can significantly disrupt sleep patterns. Adequate and restorative sleep is crucial for physical and mental health. Sleep is vital for the regulation of hormones, including those that influence mood and stress. It also contributes to cognitive function, enhances memory, and supports your immune system. Women experiencing menopause-related sleep disturbances may face an increased risk of mood disorders, fatigue, and the inability to cope with daily stressors. Prioritizing good sleep hygiene and establishing a consistent sleep routine are essential for women during this stage of their life.

Here are a few tips for optimal sleep hygiene: Stimulants, such as caffeine and nicotine prior to bedtime, can lead to increased heart rate, alertness, and difficulty winding down. Consuming these substances close to bedtime can disrupt the natural progression of sleep cycles, making it harder to fall asleep and diminishing the overall quality of rest.

If you are a smoker and have ever thought of quitting, now would be the perfect time. Smokers are more likely to have an unpleasant menopausal experience. We know that smokers have more hot flashes as they go through menopause. Smoking can also intensify the symptoms of menopause, including the intensity of the hot flashes and more difficulty sleeping. And smoking's effects linger long after hot flashes stop. Although menopause is a natural part of the aging process, smoking makes what can be expected even worse (*www.lancastergeneralhealth.org*).

Women also report that consuming alcohol increases their hot flashes and night sweats. Consuming alcohol has vasodilatory effects, which can widen blood vessels, and can potentially impact your hormone balance and contribute to symptom severity.

Nutrition also plays a key role in maintaining balance during menopause. A diet rich in essential nutrients, such as vitamins and minerals, plays a crucial role in supporting overall health. Incorporating an adequate intake of calcium and vitamin D helps maintain bone density, reducing the risk of osteoporosis – a common concern for menopausal women. Additionally, incorporating phytoestrogen-rich foods like soy, flaxseeds, and whole grains can potentially reduce your hormonal fluctuations and reduce hot flashes. Phytoestrogens are naturally occurring compounds found in plants that have a chemical structure similar to the hormone estrogen, which play a key role in the development and function of the reproductive system.

Lastly, there are medications that can be prescribed by your physician to help with your physical and mental symptoms. It is important to talk to your spouse and your doctor about what you are going through. Having a great support system is key in managing your life during this time. The list of these medications is to be used as a reference only. These are the most current medications approved by the FDA at this time.

Prescription Medications:
Veozah™ (fezolinetant): the first drug designed to treat hot flashes and indicated to reduce moderate to severe vasomotor symptoms due to menopause, a non-hormonal treatment, works by blocking neurokinin B (NKB) from binding to the kisspeptin/neurokinin B/dynorphin (KNDy) neuron that modulates neuronal activity in the thermoregulatory center
Hormone Therapies
Estrogen-only Medicines: available in a variety of dosage forms including tablets, patch, gel, vaginal or skin creams
Progestin-only Medicines in tablet form including Prometrium and Provera
Combination Estrogen and Progestin Medicines: Activella, Angeliq, Climara Pro patch, Combipatch, Femhrt, Prefest, and Prempro

Reduction of hot flashes
Antidepressants such as the Selective Serotonin Reuptake Inhibitor (SSRIs)
Clonidine
Gabapentin
Pregabalin
Oxybutynin
Bone Loss
Estrogen agonists/antagonists: Evista (raloxifene)
Bisphosphonates
Vaginal Dryness
Estrogen (vaginal cream)
Lubricants and moisturizers (over the counter)

Over The Counter (OTC):

1. Equelle® (S-equol)
2. Menoprin™
3. Nova Menostage
4. Amberen
5. Logos Nutritionals Eve's Harmony
6. Specialist Supplements MENOstage
7. Zenulife Menovax
8. Nature Made Multi for her 50+
9. Gaia Herbs Women's Balance
10. Enzymatic Therapy AM/PM Menopause Formula
11. Nutra Life Meno-Life Hot Flush Relief

CHAPTER 5

THE MENOPAUSE DIARIES
DRIED OUT

It's Thanksgiving Day and my house is full of people. Everyone is in the kitchen, and I feel like I'm going to lose my mind. My daughter decided to bake an appetizer at the last minute and took some of my oven space. I wanted to strangle her. Then, I noticed that the turkey was in the bottom oven turning brown and crispy. I opened the door and sure enough, the turkey was getting dried out. My husband decided to warm up the turkey and had the oven temperature too high. I lost it! I started yelling at him and told him the turkey was ruined. He just looked at me with a blank stare on his face and my house guests ran over to console him. I later felt terrible for yelling at him, but my hormones took over and I felt like I was out of control. That holiday felt like the movie Christmas Vacation.

Missy C., Age 52

6

HOT BUT NOT

It is 5 pm on December 31st and I am getting ready for our neighbor's annual New Year's Eve Party. Everyone in our neighborhood has been invited. I should be excited to ring in the New Year, yet all I am thinking about is my New Year's resolutions – failed ones from the previous years and the hope of starting new ones. I say to myself, *I'm going to stick to it this year. I'm more motivated now. I know I can do this.* Who was I kidding? Only myself. I have had the same resolutions for the past 5 years. I am going to be motivated to exercise and lose those unwanted pounds. Yet, each year the weight has continued to creep up.

SOLVING THE MYSTERY OF MENOPAUSE

My clothes are not only tight, they also just don't fit. All those cute outfits I used to wear to parties are now filled with dust in the spare closet, the skinny clothes closet. As I try on outfit after outfit, hoping that something will fit, I finally come to realize that it is hopeless. Nothing fits me. Everything is tight and I feel like I'm carrying a spare tire around my waist. I just want to crawl into a ball and cry myself to sleep. If only I were a bear and could hibernate through this ordeal and not come out until next year.

I then look at myself in the mirror, and I see a different version of myself. I start noticing the lines on my forehead, the gray hairs that are creeping through, and the sagging lines around my chin. *How can this be me*? I ask. Did this happen overnight? Or have I been in denial of this aging process? I soon begin to spiral downwards, into a deep, black hole. I tell myself that I am fat, I look old, and I don't deserve to go to a party and have fun!

I shed some tears with my husband and tell him how embarrassed I am to go to this party. I don't have anything fancy to wear and I just want to go to bed. Even though he reassures me that I am beautiful, and I look wonderful in the outfit that I have chosen, my emotional state has taken a nosedive. I finally agreed to go to the party, and I

CHAPTER 6

actually had a good time. I did manage to avoid having my picture taken, in fear that I would be seen as looking old and overweight.

Society today worships beauty. Every billboard, magazine cover, and television commercial show young and vibrant models that appear to be perfect in every way. They are smiling and laughing and have no physical imperfections. Technology can now erase every line, wrinkle and crease on your face. It can even shed those unwanted pounds from your photos. No wonder women feel shame and embarrassment as we start to age. Unless we succumb to botox, lasers, or go under the knife for plastic surgery, we can no longer compete with those younger than us.

I realize that harboring these negative thoughts and feelings can lead to a domino effect. As I shared in Chapter 3, there are many side effects of the hormonal changes we experience during menopause. Let's dive deeper into some of them.

It all starts with the physical effects of menopause: hot flashes, weight gain, and dry, brittle, and thinning hair and skin. These start to take a toll on our bodies and our emotions. When we start feeling old physically, we convince ourselves that we look old as well.

We start to become more emotional, cry more often, and feel anger at the simplest things. This can lead to isolating and withdrawing from friends and family. We soon find that we no longer want to go to dinner with friends or attend social events because we are too embarrassed by how we look and feel. I think to myself, *how can I go to a summer barbeque and wear shorts in public or wear a dress to a friend's wedding? I look hideous in every outfit I try on.*

> menopause contributes to feelings of shame and embarrassment.

These thoughts lead to feelings of shame – shame for the way we look, and feelings of guilt for declining invitations from our closest friends. There is a stigma surrounding menopause that contributes to these feelings of shame and embarrassment – we feel a sense of loss for our youth and our fertility. The physical and emotional symptoms, such as hot flashes, mood swings, and changes in libido, can intensify these feelings, and leave us feeling vulnerable.

The fact is most women are affected by menopause. Our hormone levels drop dramatically, and we feel the physical and emotional effects from this decline. Hot flashes are the primary symptom that women experience during

CHAPTER 6

perimenopause and menopause. Suddenly the term *hot* takes on a new connotation during this time. The term no longer implies the young, sexier version of you. It now shows its ugly face as an older, less confident version of you.

The physical symptoms of menopause are uniquely individual. I experienced most of my hot flashes primarily at night when I was sleeping. I had, on average, 30 hot flashes each night – yes, I counted them. I would wake up with this feeling of heat, which started at my feet and slowly moved up towards my head. It began as a subtle warmth, intensifying into an inferno that left me drenched in perspiration and my heart racing.

Night after night, this persistent intrusion of hot flashes and night sweats disrupted my peaceful slumber, which transformed my haven of sleep into an agonizing battleground. Each night became a struggle to find relief amidst the unpredictable surges of heat. The ordeal not only affected the quantity, but also the quality of my sleep. The overwhelming warmth robbed me of precious moments of rest, and left me fatigued and irritable during the day.

The mental and physical exhaustion was disrupting my life. I was working 12-hour shifts as a nurse at the time and found that I was having a hard time performing my job effectively. I became irritable with my coworkers and even my patients. Numerous cups of coffee were not helping to keep me awake. They only made me more anxious and jittery. There were times that I literally thought I was going to have a nervous breakdown.

What happened to this vibrant young woman that I used to be? I felt like she disappeared overnight with no warning. I had so many unanswered questions and soon found myself angry and confused. I was angry with myself and with the world. Why was I not prepared for this change in my life? The bigger question is why was I not prepared for it? Nobody wants to talk about it.

My mother never sat me down and had a conversation with me about this subject. Schools teach children the facts of life and even about menstruation, but nothing about preparing for menopause. It is treated like a hidden secret, locked away in a closet until we reach our 50s. As a child, I remember overhearing conversations about the crazy aunt that went off the deep end and had to go to a special doctor and get on medicine. I found out many years later that my dear aunt was going through menopause and felt like she was going insane. Apparently, her doctor put her on *medicine to make her feel better.* My aunt was soon back to normal

CHAPTER 6

and the secret whispering about her behind her back suddenly vanished.

Some cultures view menopause as a change of seasons and even call it a rite of passage. I must admit, there are days that I embrace this change and then there are days that I question it. There are times that I feel as though I am being tormented by these changes. I long for my soft and vibrant hair again. I want my skin to be smooth and hydrated. *And why have my eyebrows stopped growing?* I feel like I have aged 10 years overnight.

There are times I feel guilty for having these feelings, but why? Why should we feel guilty for wanting to be young and beautiful again? For me, the answer is simple. I have always been told that the women in my family have always aged gracefully. I had intended to do the same until signs of aging came upon me. I simply was not prepared for this.

So, what can we do about it? I can tell you with certainty that I am going to fight the aging process for as long as I can. I am going to do whatever I can to age as gracefully as my elders have. I have chosen to not use cosmetic enhancements at this stage of my life. I do keep an open mind and may choose this path later in life. These treatments may be right for you. Only you can make that decision. If having these procedures improves your emotional well-being, then go ahead without judgment. This is what is so great about living in our society today. We have so many options at our fingertips to help us look and feel more vibrant.

There are many ways to help yourself stay young and healthy mentally, emotionally and physically. We cannot allow these negative stereotypes of menopausal women continue. We must stand up and fight. No more giving in and taking the easy way out. Stop picking up fast food on the way home and start making healthy meals for yourself. No more sitting on the couch watching television for hours every evening. Do something about it. The change must come from within.

A simple step to change your emotions and your physical health is to take care of your body, inside and out. Only you have the power over what you put into your body and what you choose to see, speak, or hear. Nobody can take that away from you. It is never too late to start improving your health. Starting with one small change will eventually lead to larger changes, and before you know it, you will feel like your old self again. So, what are you waiting for?

There is an old saying by the late Henry Ford, *"If you always do what you've always done, you'll always get what you've always*

CHAPTER 6

got." This is the perfect time to make lasting changes that will enable you to embrace this season of life. You no longer have to feel tired, overwhelmed, and exhausted. You have the right to feel happy, energized, and full of life. You may be asking yourself, *where do I start*? The next chapter will help you get started on your journey to a healthier and happier you.

THE TOILET DIARIES

One benefit of aging is that our body becomes less forgiving, and sends us messages about areas we can change to improve our health. Observing these messages becomes especially important when we go through menopause. One of the best places to look for feedback on our health is the toilet! Yes, the toilet. There are two experiences from my time in nursing school that illustrate this point.

One day, our chemistry teacher was lecturing on the different chemicals in the body, specifically in the gut or the gastrointestinal system. She shocked us all when she asked us to share with the class what our stool looked like. Most of the students in class began to whisper and giggle. Nobody wanted to answer this strange and embarrassing question. Everyone goes to the bathroom, so why is it such a taboo subject?

Our instructor began to call on students, one by one, forcing them to answer or at least comment on her question. She then gave us a homework assignment. We had to go home and look at our bowel movements and record the size, shape, and color. This sounded horrendous to my 30-year-old self. I did not want to look in the toilet at my human waste. I just wanted to flush it down and forget about it.

Our instructor began to explain how a diet rich in high fiber, plant-based foods can give you the ultimate bathroom experience. She then proceeded to tell us that our feces will float in the toilet when we have consumed adequate amounts of fiber. This is a sign that our gut is healthy and working properly. I looked at the smirk on her face and thought, *Is this lady for real?*

I had never really looked in the toilet before. Well, I have looked, but really never paid attention to the contents in the toilet bowl. I thought to myself, *poop is poop* – yes, that dirty word nobody wants to talk about. I felt that I had the same type of bowel movements most of my life. Or have I?

CHAPTER 7

This got the wheels turning in my brain. I started to dive a little deeper into the subject.

I went home that evening and, as the obedient student I was, did exactly as I was told. When it was time to have a bowel movement, I went into the bathroom, and eagerly waited to see the contents in the toilet. I looked down at the contents, and to my surprise, I did not see any flotation. There, before my very own eyes, was this lifeless piece of excrement, waiting to be flushed down the toilet. I was not sure how to react. Should I laugh, or should I be worried? Was my teacher joking with us, or was my diet really that horrible? I decided to experiment with my diet before the next lecture.

I have eaten the same types of food for most of my life. I eat a primarily plant-based diet with fish and dairy on occasion. I go to the bathroom like clockwork, at the same time every day. When I am eating completely plant based, I have 2-3 bowel movements a day. They are robust and healthy if there is such a thing. I did notice that when I omitted fish and dairy from my diet and increased my fiber, my stool did indeed float. I was shocked and amazed. How did I go through life and never pay attention to this?

I was pleased to write my statement and I eagerly shared my findings with my entire class at the next lecture. Listening to my peers share their own stories, or as I like to call them, *The Toilet Diaries*, made me question my own dietary and lifestyle choices. I started to keep a record of what I ate and how it affected my stool. I found that when I increased my intake of fruits and vegetables and omitted animal products, I would have a perfect elimination every time.

Why is it so important to have a healthy digestive tract? A healthy digestive tract is crucial for overall well-being because it plays a central role in the absorption of nutrients, the elimination of waste, and maintaining the balance of your gut microbiome. The gut microbiome refers to the diverse community of microorganisms, including bacteria, viruses, fungi, and other microbes, that inhabit the gastrointestinal tract. The gut microbiome is a complex ecosystem that plays a crucial role in various aspects of health, including digestion, metabolism, immune function, and even mental health.

The composition of the gut microbiome can be influenced by factors such as diet, antibiotic use, genetics, and environmental exposures. Maintaining a diverse and balanced microbiome can be beneficial for overall health. Here are a few ways to maintain a healthy gut:

- Eat foods rich in fiber, such as fruits, vegetables, nuts, and seeds.
- Eat foods rich in probiotics such as yogurt, sauerkraut, miso, kimchi, and other fermented foods.
- Stay hydrated by drinking plenty of water, which supports the growth of beneficial bacteria.
- Limit artificial sweeteners.
- Limit antibiotic use/overuse, which can disrupt the gut microbiome.
- Exercise regularly.
- Get plenty of restful sleep.
- Limit your intake of processed foods.
- Manage stress – practice meditation, yoga, and deep breathing exercises.
- Consider a probiotic.

Now let's talk about the negative effects of an imbalanced digestive system. An unhealthy gut can manifest itself in several ways that can impact your physical and mental well-being. Common signs include digestive issues such as bloating, gas, constipation, diarrhea, and heartburn. Skin problems like acne and eczema, as well as food intolerances and frequent infections, may also be linked to an imbalance in your gut. Mood disorders such as anxiety and depression are also influenced by your gut health.

Stool consistency and buoyancy can be influenced by various factors, and while floating stool is considered normal, it's important to note that individual variations exist. Dietary factors can influence your stool. Foods rich in fiber, such as fruits, vegetables, and whole grains can cause your stool to float since adding fiber may increase gas production, leading to buoyancy. If you are experiencing persistent digestive issues or have concerns about your stool, it's recommended to consult with a healthcare provider.

Once I graduated nursing school and began working as a nurse, I realized how important gut health was to maintain optimal health. One of the key assessments for patients in the hospital was asking them about their bowel health. Each shift, patients would be asked the same questions: *Did you have a bowel movement today? How often do you have them? What do they look like?* Having a healthy gut is just as important as having good blood pressure.

CHAPTER 7

When I asked my older patients about their bowel movements, I noticed that they were somewhat obsessed with their bowel health. They made sure they stayed regular and many of them even supplemented with stool softeners and fiber. I couldn't understand their obsession. I used to joke about being obsessed with my stool when I got older. I thought, *No way am I going to be like this.* Well, here I am, 20 years later, to tell you that yes, I am obsessed with my gut health and for lack of a better word, my poop!

That solitary homework assignment and what I observed when taking care of my patients, has led me on a journey of studying gut health and its importance on our lives. I have journeyed down this rabbit hole, and I cannot go back. Science is now studying the gastrointestinal tract and its positive effects on our body and our mind.

These studies of the gastrointestinal tract are called *The Gut-Brain-Axis*. It is also called our *Second Brain*. So, what exactly is this phenomenon everyone has been talking about? I will try to sum it up in a nutshell. This *Second Brain* is also called the enteric nervous system (ENS). The ENS is made up of two thin layers that contain more than 100 million nerve cells. These cells line your gastrointestinal tract that runs from your esophagus all the way down to your rectum. The *Second Brain* in your gut, or the ENS, communicates directly with the brain in your head. This is called the brain-gut connection or gut brain link (*www.webmd.com*).

Your gut's main connection to the brain is the vagus nerve. This nerve also controls messages that are sent to the heart, lungs, and other organs. Additionally, hormones and other neurotransmitters travel along *The Gut-Brain-Axis* to send messages chemically (*www.webmd.com*).

> If your gut is healthy then your mind and brain are healthy.

These messages that are carried back and forth from the gut are highly affected by your gut microbiome. Your microbiome essentially are all the bacteria, viruses, and fungi that are living inside of you. It makes sense to say that if your gut is healthy then your mind and brain are healthy.

This gut-brain connection goes both ways. Many of our emotions are tied to our gut. A troubled intestine can send signals to the brain, just as a troubled brain can send signals to the gut. When you are feeling stressed out or anxious, these emotions wreak havoc on your gastrointestinal system. This disruption in your gut then disrupts your hormones, which often leads to more anxiety and stress. This

CHAPTER 7

further affects your gut. This is a vicious cycle that can lead you down a path of multiple doctor visits and unwanted and unnecessary prescriptions.

Here is a good example of how this works. Remember how your stomach starts to flutter when you see a commercial for your favorite food or soft drink? Or sitting in the movie theater seeing ads for popcorn? These thoughts of eating can release the stomach's juices before your food even gets there. Your mouth starts to water, and your brain tells you that you must go buy popcorn! Or how about that big speech you must give in front of your peers? You start getting those butterflies in your stomach, you feel anxious, and your hands start to sweat. This is *The Gut-Brain-Axis* working together. These are powerful reminders of how our body systems are made to work synergistically.

Your gut also plays an important role in producing Serotonin and Dopamine. Research now suggests that approximately 50% of Dopamine and 90% of Serotonin are made in our guts. Serotonin is often referred to as the feel-good neurotransmitter. It is crucial in the overall health of our brain and our emotions.

By recognizing the delicate connection between the gut and the brain and making your gut health a priority, you can improve cognitive function and your emotional well-being. This can be one of the easiest things you can do for your overall health. Only *you* can control what goes into your body. Nobody else can tell you what and how much to eat or drink, or even dictate how much sleep you get. Empower yourself by taking control of your actions. This can be a transformative journey that begins with self-awareness and a commitment to personal growth. Now that you are ready to make lasting changes to improve your health, start with your gut.

> *Twenty years from now you will be more disappointed by the things you didn't do than by the things you did.*
>
> —MARK TWAIN

8
TREAT YOURSELF

Finally, a chapter dedicated to *YOU*. Are you the typical woman who puts everyone and everything else before you? Do you spend most of your day juggling your work, home, and life? Don't fret, this chapter will provide you with suggestions to guide you on a self-care journey. There are some routines that have helped me tremendously in this phase of life and I want to share them with you.

There are many ways to help ease the emotional and physical discomfort that comes with menopause. Incorporating self-care is often overlooked but can be extremely important. It can give you that extra edge that you may be missing to manage your symptoms. But often these discomforts are distracting you from taking care of yourself.

Most physicians suggest either prescription or over-the-counter medications to help alleviate your symptoms, but these alone may not be sufficient. (Refer to Chapter 5 for a list of FDA approved drugs currently on the market.) It is crucial to educate yourself, take action, and make informed choices regarding your health. A great way to start is partnering with your spouse and your physician. In doing so, it empowers you to actively participate in the management of your own health.

> Educate yourself, take action, and make informed choices regarding your health.

An example of the importance of a multi-pronged approach is someone who wants to lose weight. Taking weight-loss pills alone is not going to help you achieve the ultimate goal of losing weight. One must also consider exercising, eating healthier foods, and monitoring your food portions. The same goes for menopause. We must make time to take care of our body, mind, and soul. I love pampering myself. I love bubble baths, candles, and listening to soft music. I take advantage of cold, rainy days by putting on comfy pajamas and reading a good book, listening to music, or simply

CHAPTER 8

watching some of my favorite movies. So why don't I do this on a more regular basis? What a good question!

The problem is making the time to do this. Just like anything else in life, if we do not schedule time for ourselves on our calendars, it will never get done. We tend to put ourselves last. Most people take better care of their cars and houses than their bodies. We schedule our oil changes and tire rotations, get our house painted and manicure our lawns. We clean our houses, eat our dinner, and then veg-out on the couch each night because we are so exhausted from all of these *have-to's* from the day.

But what about us? We should be our #1 priority. If we do not take care of ourselves first, we cannot take care of our family, and we are more than likely not doing our jobs to our full potential.

This can lead to grumpy children, frustrated spouses, and potentially putting our jobs at risk. We tend to go through life on autopilot. We go to bed exhausted each night and then wake up just as tired as when we laid down the night before. We hit the snooze button several times, then grudgingly get out of bed, start our mundane chores and then proceed to force a smile on our face in an attempt to start the day. We drink several cups of coffee to wake up, make poor food choices throughout our day, and complain that we are exhausted and just don't feel good. Well, no wonder we feel tired and run-down. We have gotten used to running on empty, day after day, year after year.

Learning to take care of yourself each day can enrich your life in more ways than you can imagine. Incorporating self-care into your daily routine not only soothes the mind and body, but it can also soothe the soul. The first step is setting an intention to begin loving yourself again. For me, the key was to start with one small routine weekly and then gradually work towards daily practice.

> The first step is setting an intention to begin loving yourself again.

A good way to start your day is with positive affirmations. Smile in the mirror and tell yourself that you are going to have a great day today. Continue your day practicing gratefulness for the small things in your life. It can be your children, pets, spouse or even just the field of flowers you see on your way to work each day. You can be grateful for having a roof over your head and food on your table. There are many free resources online and even in your public library on positive affirmations to help guide you. (One example is a book written by Louise L. Hay, *Meditations to Heal Your Life*.

CHAPTER 8

Other titles are listed on her website: *www.louisehay.com.)* This can feel foreign to you at first, but with daily practice it will start to feel as normal as brushing your teeth.

For those of you who meditate, this can be a great start (or an end) to your day. If meditation is not something that appeals to you, then sitting in a quiet space and reflecting on your day can be advantageous. It allows for introspection on your day, week, and even your life. Taking a walk in nature can also provide the peace and solitude that your mind and body have been craving.

I find that when I force myself to go outside and sit or walk in nature, I feel a sense of peace come over me. You will gain a new perspective on life and have the ability to realign your priorities. It can feel like a weight has been lifted off your shoulders. The simple act of walking outside, breathing in the fresh air, listening to the leaves sway gently in the breeze, and the birds happily chirping can elevate your mood in an instant.

Walking is also an excellent way to get in some low impact exercise for the day. It increases the blood flow to your heart, lungs and even your brain. This increase of blood flow to your brain can improve your cognition and even boost your mood. Walking is also a great way to increase muscle mass and bone density. Menopause can be associated with a natural decrease in your estrogen levels, which leads to a decrease in bone mass density, overall muscle mass and strength, and can also increase your visceral fat mass. So, what are you waiting for? Get out there in nature and start walking.

Here are a few other tidbits to help you along your journey. Limiting your caffeine intake to one cup per day, and not drinking it after lunchtime, can help prevent insomnia. You may also want to explore alternative therapies to help reduce symptoms and improve our overall well-being such as acupuncture, massage therapy, meditation, and deep breathing exercises. Essential oils can also be a great asset to your arsenal of feel-good remedies.

Acupuncture has been known to help with hot flashes, night sweats, insomnia, pain, mood swings, anxiety, fatigue, and vaginal dryness. I receive acupuncture on a regular basis for my hormonal health and my overall enjoyment. I get to lay on the table in a soft, candlelit room with soft music playing in the background. I close my eyes and inhale the relaxing fragrance of essential oils that are floating throughout the room. There is no pain – I only feel total and complete relaxation for 30-45 minutes. I even

CHAPTER 8

find that I drift off to sleep during my session and wake up feeling totally refreshed.

Another way to help improve your mood naturally is to start making healthier food choices. I am not here to tell you to stop eating certain foods, but I can tell you that the more processed the food, the unhealthier it is. These types of fast foods have chemicals in them that are considered hormone disruptors. They alter your hormones even more than menopause alone. This can lead to more symptoms such as hot flashes, lethargy, and weight gain. A good rule of thumb is to add one new food into your diet each week. Make it a healthy choice. Try experimenting with these new foods by making a new recipe each week. The more you add foods to your meals that are good for you, the more your body will crave these foods, and you will naturally start omitting the foods that are less healthy.

> Diet and lifestyle can also influence your transition into all stages of menopause.

Diet and lifestyle factors can also influence your transition into all stages of menopause. It is important to try and incorporate healthy, plant-based, organic foods into your daily routine. These foods help decrease inflammation, improve your gut health, increase your energy levels, improve sleep, and can help elevate your mood. New studies have come out reporting that a healthy diet is associated with significantly lower risks of Alzheimer's disease and depression (Dr. Daniel G. Amen, *Unleash the Power of the Female Brain*).

I'm not here to tell you to stop eating animal products, but I am encouraging you to incorporate more plant-based foods into your diet. Many of us are so busy that we tend to eat out at restaurants more often and choose prepackaged foods due to time constraints. These foods have many unhealthy ingredients in them. They may be convenient now, but in 20 years, they will be rather inconvenient. Eating unhealthy foods will eventually take its toll on the body, showing up as obesity, cancers, and many other diseases later in life. Don't wait until it's too late – start making smarter choices today. Your body will not only thank you now, but also well into your 60s, 70s, and even your 80s.

When you start feeling good, you will want to continue this journey. You may start losing weight, your clothes may fit you better, and you will gain a new-self confidence in yourself. Now you may decide that you want to start walking or joining a gym. You will find an inner strength in yourself.

CHAPTER 8

This can be an invigorating feeling. Your body and your mind will thank you for making these changes.

A great way to clear your head from your daily stressors is to sit quietly each evening, before you go to bed, and write down in a journal or on a notepad, everything from the day that was left unfinished. Write down what needs to be done the next day. Doing this helps clear your mind of all the tasks that are unfinished. When you get up the next day, you have your list of things that need to be done. This will allow you to conquer the day more efficiently.

There are many ways to help ease your transition during this time. For some women, the physical symptoms tend to overshadow the mental and emotional ones. Hot flashes tend to be the most prevalent symptom that women report. Here are a few strategies to help ease some of these physical manifestations. Turn down your thermostat at night. You don't need to freeze out your family, but having a cooler temperature at night will allow you to have a more restful sleep and help prevent numerous hot flashes. Dress in layers during the day. When a hot flash comes on, you will be able to easily take off that outer layer. Avoid alcohol and hot and spicy foods. Take a vacation somewhere cool instead of the tropics. This will ensure that you will be able to enjoy yourself. Drink lots of fluids, preferably water. Talk to your physician about possible supplements that may help ease your symptoms. For your emotional and mental wellbeing, explore meditation or deep breathing exercises. Practicing these strategies helped ease my symptoms dramatically.

> It takes 21 days to make a habit and 90 days to make it a permanent lifestyle change.

The world we live in is fast paced. We allow the mundane chores of life to get in our way and forget to take time to slow down. I set daily reminders to ensure that I consistently prioritize self-care. With daily practice, you can make these simple changes part of your permanent routine. Research states that it takes 21 days to make a habit and 90 days to make it a permanent lifestyle change (*www.activeiron.com*).

Lastly, learn to relax and enjoy your life. Take time to read, take bubble-baths, play games with your grandkids, eat that piece of pie, and laugh. Life is meant to be enjoyed every day. Don't wait until tomorrow to live your life – start right now. Don't let anything or anyone stand in your way. You have earned every wrinkle and gray hair. Wear them proudly. This is the time to stand tall and let your inner-goddess shine. Let the world know that you are

CHAPTER 8

invincible. This little thing called menopause is not going to stop you. Allow it to make you stronger and more resilient. Now – go out into the world and be *amazing*!

THE MENOPAUSE DIARIES
AN IRRATIONAL ESCAPE

I was tired and frustrated. My husband was always working, and I was home all day with three kids. I don't know what hit me, but I had it in my mind that he was having an affair. It started as a small thought. I let it repeat in my mind over and over again. Suddenly, I was convinced that this thought was true. What am I going to do? This inner voice said, "I'll show him. I'm going to leave." So, I packed up the car with all three children in tow, and headed out. Where to? I didn't even know. I just knew I had to get out of this situation. Before I could leave, my husband pulled into the drive, bewilderment in his eyes and asked, "What are you doing?" I told him I was taking the kids and getting out of here.

Rhonda R., Age 36

PART 3
MENTAL MENOPAUSE

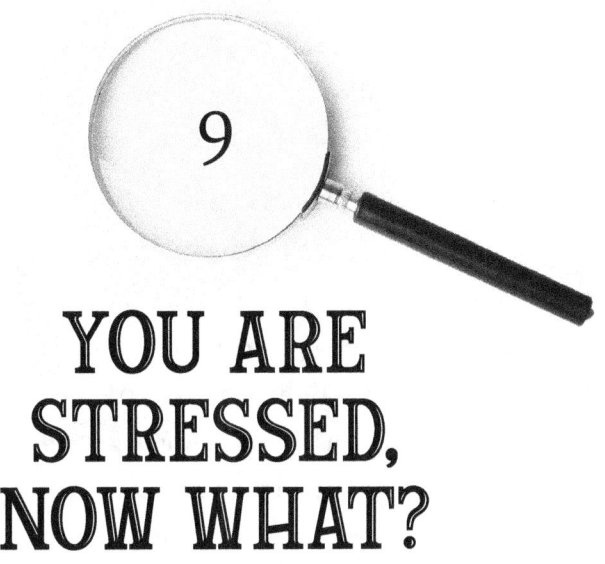

YOU ARE STRESSED, NOW WHAT?

It's 5:30 in the morning – the alarm goes off – you hit snooze. Five minutes later, the alarm goes off again. You roll yourself out of bed, go directly to the bathroom and begin your daily routine. You are tired, exhausted, and not ready to face the day. You go to the kitchen to start the coffee, feed the cats, and then rush back to the bedroom to finish getting ready. You have your daily bathroom ritual where you sit for 5 minutes and check emails and social media. You finish, check to see if your poop floats, and then you rush back to the kitchen. You grab your lunch and your coffee and head out the door, knowing that you are running late – again.

Does this sound familiar? Our society has taught us that we need to move at a fast pace, multi-task, and be in go-mode almost constantly. There is little room for rest and quiet contemplation. We order our coffee online and pick it up at the drive-thru, we have our groceries delivered to our door, and most of us are either working 12-hour days or are on-call 24/7. Neither our bodies or our minds are meant to be in this constant state of stress or chaos.

Stress is a normal reaction that helps us deal with our daily challenges. There are two types of stress: positive and negative. Positive stress is short-term and can inspire and motivate you, allowing you to focus your energy. It can lead to feelings of fulfillment and excitement. For instance, when you are preparing to interview for a new job, your heart starts racing, your palms begin to sweat, and your hands start to tremble. How about that first date that is coming up? You stress about what you are going to wear, and you rehearse the evening dialogue in your head so that you will be prepared for any unexpected questions. These are considered positive stress reactions.

CHAPTER 9

Negative stress, however, is the kind that wears you out, leaves you jittery and is harmful to your health. This type of stress can be perceived as unhealthy or threatening and can lead to anxiety and depression. Where I live, there are bears. Lots and lots of bears. They are in my yard daily during the summer months. We have learned to cohabitate together. Now, if I'm working in my yard and turn around to find a bear hovering over me, I'm more than likely going to instantly enter into a state of panic. This is what we call negative stress. Our bodies have a built-in protection system to help us in these times of stress. They are under the influence of our sympathetic nervous system (SNS).

The SNS signals our *fight or flight response* to kick in. Our body gives us what we need to survive. Our hearts begin to race, our pulse and respirations go up, we begin to sweat, and our pupils dilate, so that we can run or fight. A normal stress response should only last for a few minutes, or until danger is gone, and our bodies can then go back to their normal resting state. The problem today is that we are in regular states of stress with no real danger. We are attempting to work, raise a family, cook, clean, go to school functions and somehow try and take time for ourselves – but that time never comes. This constant state of stress is literally killing us because our bodies are not meant to have the stress response and the accompanying hormones all the time.

Medical research estimates that as much as 90 percent of illness and disease is stress-related. Stress can interfere with your physical functioning and bodily processes. High blood pressure, cardiovascular disease, and heart disease have been linked to stress factors (www.nasdonline.org).

Our stress response is meant to be short and infrequent, but our lives leave us in a constant state of stress. Over time, our bodies adapt and build up a tolerance to these stress responses and this can have adverse effects on your body. The increase in your blood pressure and pulse can eventually lead to a heart attack. The constant knot in your stomach can cause gastrointestinal issues like nausea, vomiting or even acid reflux. You may also experience mood issues such as depression, anxiety and have trouble sleeping. You may have a loss of libido and absent or irregular menstrual cycles.

> There are three stages of stress: the alarm stage, resistance stage and exhaustion stage.

Research has shown that there are three stages of stress: the alarm stage, resistance stage and exhaustion stage. The first stage is the fight or flight state. This is our panic mode. The second or resistance stage is when our body attempts to normalize. We cannot fully relax because the next stressor is right around the corner. Finally, the exhaustion stage is where most of us are today. We have been in a constant state of stress that our body can no longer fight. This is when our body starts to shut down. We begin to feel signs of fatigue, burnout, depression and anxiety, and a decrease in our stress tolerance (*www.healthline.com*).

So while our sympathetic nervous system is for times of stress and crisis (flight or flight), our parasympathetic nervous system helps maintain normal body functions and conserve physical resources. Once a threat has passed, this system will slow the heart rate and breathing, reduce blood flow to muscles, and constrict the pupils. This allows the body to return to a normal resting state (*www.verywellmind.com*).

> "We live too short and die too long."
>
> WALTER BORTZ, MD

Unfortunately, most of us are never able to fully return to this more relaxed state. We tend to go about our day-to-day business, putting out fires and going through life as if nothing were wrong. Walter Bortz, MD says, "We live too short and die too long." This is a profound statement. We never fully live; and when it is time to die, we are reminded of all the physical and mental effects from the stressful life we have lived. We suffer needlessly from all the stressors in our life that could have been easily prevented.

So how do we know if our stress levels are too high? Pay attention to your behavior and your body. Do you yell at your kids or fight with your spouse? Are you short-tempered at work? Do you feel run-down or tired all the time? These are some of the physical symptoms that may present themselves as signs of stress. The more serious symptoms are high blood pressure, an increase in your pulse, headaches, and even sleeping too much or too little.

Chronic stress can affect every body system. This can cause you to eat unhealthy foods and make poor food choices. This inevitably compromises your immune system, diminishing its ability to function optimally and leaving you more susceptible to infections and illnesses. A compromised immune system can result in increased vulnerability to infections, prolonged illness recovery, and heightened risk of various health complications. You may find that you are more prone to colds and your allergies flare up more often. More severe side effects of stress can increase your risk for heart disease, stroke, weight gain,

CHAPTER 9

memory issues, sleep problems and even depression, just to name a few (*www.mayoclinic.org*).

When I get stressed, I tend to eat more comfort foods – the foods that bring back good memories of my childhood. Macaroni and cheese, pizza, mashed potatoes and gravy are just a few. In fact, I crave most carbs! These foods are not completely unhealthy, but they certainly do not help keep the weight off or provide the energy I need to get through the day.

Many people who are under stress have the opposite effect of overeating. Some people under daily stress lose their appetite. This can be dangerous as well. For some, your body is in a constant *fight or flight mode,* causing your body to not recognize that you need food. This can lead to digestive problems, deplete your energy stores, and possibly lead to an eating disorder.

Menopause can alter your mood, so consuming foods that improve your frame of mind is key. Include foods containing Omega-3 such as salmon, sardines, tuna, walnuts, edamame, chia, and flax seeds, which are all beneficial not only to your brain health, but also your body as well. Omega-3 may help decrease inflammation in the body, lower cholesterol, and improve eye health. It may also help with depression and anxiety and keep your skin healthy, preventing premature aging and safeguarding against sun damage (*www.healthline.com*).

Your ability to recognize that you are stressed is the first step to helping yourself. Talk to your family, friends, and even your co-workers. You will be surprised at how much people really do care and are willing to help you. You do not have to suffer alone. Life can be stressful as is, but going through menopause can exacerbate that stress. It is important to be able to recognize your symptoms early on so that you can live a happy and fulfilling life.

When I was in my early 50s, I was stressed about my family; I was unhappy in my job; I was gaining weight; and I just felt lost. I found myself eating foods that I normally do not eat. I was tired, so I started eating out more often. I was drinking too much coffee to boost my energy, and I was using stress as an excuse to have two glasses of wine each evening. Adding these bad habits to my stress made me more stressed. This was becoming a vicious pattern of unhealthy habits.

Even as a mental health nurse, I did not recognize the symptoms right away. I blamed everyone and everything for my unhappiness. I felt like I was trapped in this life with

CHAPTER 9

no way out. There was a point where I felt so lost and alone that I just wanted to give everything up. I told my husband that I just wanted to quit my job and run away to a secluded place where nobody would find me.

I finally recognized that something had to change. I decided to write a list of all the things for which I was grateful, and another list of things that I wanted to change. I decided to find solutions for the things that I could change immediately. The first thing on my list of stressors was my job. I decided to open up to my boss and explain that I was feeling unhappy and overwhelmed. I did not want to leave my job, but was unhappy in my current position. She was happy that I opened up to her, and I was able to change to a different department. This simple change made a drastic improvement in my stress levels and I started enjoying my job again. If only I had done this months ago.

I then decided that I was going to start cooking my meals at home again and limit my eating out. I reduced my caffeine and alcohol consumption. It was too hot to walk in Florida, so I decided to use my pool and do exercises everyday after work. This not only helped me lose weight, but I also felt healthier on the inside as well. My mood lifted and I began to enjoy life to its fullest again.

One of the best stress management tools is physical activity. You don't have to join an expensive gym or buy sophisticated equipment. Walking is a simple, inexpensive, and low impact exercise that can be done by almost anyone and anywhere. You can walk in a park, the mall, or just take the stairs instead of the elevator. Walking is a great way to improve your overall sense of emotional well-being.

> One of the best stress management tools is physical activity.

The simple act of walking or swimming are some of the best ways to get a full body workout. Gardening, cleaning your house, taking the stairs instead of the elevator, are all good examples of getting in your daily exercise. You can even do squats or lunges on your lunch break. This will get your heart pumping!

Here are some of the physiologic benefits of exercise: decreased levels of tension, decrease in overall body fat, an increase in your oxygen levels that can elevate your mood, and a decrease in depression and anxiety. Sleep is also improved, which increases your energy levels, improves your immunity, decreases your cortisol levels and increases your endorphins.

CHAPTER 9

Endorphins are hormones that are released when your body feels pain or stress. They are produced in your brain and act as messengers in your body. Endorphins are produced to help relieve pain, reduce stress and improve mood. Endorphins can be boosted by exercising, eating, having sex, getting a massage and many other ways (www.my.clevelandclinic.org).

A great side effect of walking is spending time outside in nature. Smell the flowers or the fresh, fallen leaves on the ground. Watch squirrels jump from branch to branch. Listen to the trees sway in the wind. Block everything out and just take it all in. Get up a little earlier in the morning, or turn off the television at night. Just 15 minutes of fresh air can help alleviate your anxiety and stress from the day. You will feel refreshed and energized and will look forward to doing it again tomorrow.

Another great stress reliever is journaling. Journaling can reduce stress by helping individuals prioritize problems, fears, and concerns. Symptoms can be tracked daily and can help you recognize your negative thoughts, behaviors and even your triggers. The act of journaling can provide an opportunity for you to take repressed thoughts from an unconscious level to the conscious level. This can allow you to control and organize these negative thoughts. By transferring your thoughts to paper, you can potentially avoid future stressful situations.

A great way to get started is finding a simple notebook, a piece of paper, or you can buy a pretty journal from the bookstore. I find it useful to journal before I go to bed in the evenings. I write down all the things or events that caused me stress for the day. I then write down all my to-dos for the next day. I think of a game plan of how I will tackle that list and then I put my journal down in the kitchen. The simple act of purging all these unfinished thoughts can help you relax and enjoy a peaceful night's rest. No more worrying about all the have-to's for tomorrow.

Breathing techniques are another way to help reduce stress and anxiety. They can offer various physical, mental, and emotional benefits. Here are some of the key advantages:

- Stress reduction
- Improved focus and concentration
- Decreased anxiety and elevated mood
- Improved sleep
- Improved lung capacity
- Reduced blood pressure
- Distracted pain sensations

CHAPTER 9

- A bridge between the mind and body
- A greater awareness of the present moment

You can go online and find several types of breathing exercises that are available. Find one that is easy for you to do. If you find them difficult to follow, simply close your eyes and just breathe. It really is that simple. Here is an example of a simple breathing exercise:

1. Choose a comfortable seated position.
2. Breathe in and out through your nose.
3. Count during each inhale and exhale to make sure they are even in duration. Alternatively, choose a word or short phrase to repeat during each inhale and exhale.
4. You can add a slight pause for breath retention after each inhale and exhale if you feel comfortable. (Normal breathing involves a natural pause.)
5. Continue practicing a breathing exercise for at least 5 minutes.

Menopause can wreak havoc on your body, your brain, and even your emotions. We experience highs and lows, from happy to sad, to stressed and overwhelmed. There may be days that you feel like you are going crazy, and you cannot see a way out. You may feel hopeless and depressed. I am here to tell you that there is hope – there is a way out. The suggestions in this chapter will help you tackle menopause with grace and dignity.

It is important to learn how to manage your stress before it becomes out of control. Humans have an innate ability to recognize stress, yet we don't see it in ourselves until it is too late. Unmanaged stress leads to long term side effects such as anxiety and depression that could manifest into physical symptoms such as high blood pressure, digestive issues, and even memory impairment, just to name a few. Learning stress management techniques will help you realize you are not going crazy.

> *The mind and body are not separate.*
> *What affects one affects the other.*
> —AUTHOR UNKNOWN

10

YOU ARE NOT CRAZY

Menopause can make us feel crazy. Many of the physical symptoms of menopause can lead to mental symptoms that can be debilitating. During menopause, when your body experiences a sudden decrease in estrogen, progesterone, and other hormones, your mood and cognitive function are affected. This can result in increased anxiety and sleep disturbances. All these changes have the potential to lead to clinical depression.

When our cognitive function is affected, we may experience "brain fog." We have trouble thinking clearly, and we forget things easily, like where the keys are or what we need at the grocery store. You may notice at work that your attention-span has shortened and that you cannot concentrate on your work. Your boss is continually calling you into the office, possibly even reprimanding you for your lack of attention. If your boss is caring, he or she may ask you if something is going on in your life.

> Women are more likely to experience a depressive episode during menopause.

Many women either lose their jobs or quit during this time of their life. The emotional stress and increased anxiety start affecting the ability to perform daily tasks. The pressure is just too much. We experience rapid mood swings, laughing one minute then crying the next. We may even snap at our spouse or co-workers for no reason. All of this is related to depression and, in fact, one study showed that women are two to four times more likely to experience a major depressive episode during menopause than at other times in their lives (*www.chicagoobgyn.com*).

It is important to realize that menopause can exacerbate any pre-existing mental health issues that you may have, such as bipolar or schizophrenia (*www.chicagoobgyn.com*). It can also make us more susceptible to developing a mental illness. This is why it is so important to recognize the

CHAPTER 10

symptoms, communicate your feelings, and seek out professional help. Recognizing your symptoms is key. Once you realize what is going on with your body, you can begin taking steps to combat your manifestations. Communicating to your spouse, co-workers and even your boss is crucial. If they understand what you are going through, they will be more sympathetic and willing to help you on your journey. If you feel that your communication is not effective at relieving your symptoms, please seek out some of the many resources that are available for you.

Making lifestyle changes such as improving your diet, exercising, getting enough sleep, and even meditating can be quite powerful to reduce what you are experiencing. You may even choose psychotherapy, hormone replacement therapy, and even Cognitive Behavioral Therapy (CBT). Ask your doctor for a baseline hormone panel in your 30s and repeat every five years to see where you are in the menopause timeline. Starting early can help alleviate many years of mental, emotional, and physical symptoms. If they do not agree, find another doctor, or order tests online. You will be amazed at how many blood tests you can do yourself at home. Please have a physician review these results so that you can fully understand the results.

You should also check with your human resources department to see if you have an employee assistance program (EAP). They can help direct you to a list of therapists that are available for you through your job. Many of these are low cost, requiring only a co-pay. There are also local mental health services available in your area as well as private therapists.

> There is a stigma in our country regarding mental health services.

There is a stigma in our country regarding mental health services. Many people who think that going to therapy means you are *crazy* or *suicidal*. This way of thinking is absurd. We have a physical each year to make sure our body and organ systems are functioning properly, so why not have a mental health check-up as well? Be honest when you are explaining how you feel. Don't allow anyone to downplay your feelings or symptoms. Each woman has her own unique experience with menopause. Be an advocate for yourself and for other women. If you don't like what your therapist or doctor says, then fire them and go find another one that will listen to you.

Another form of psychotherapy is CBT. It is a type of talk therapy. CBT helps you become aware of inaccurate or negative thinking so you can view challenging situations more

CHAPTER 10

clearly and respond to them in a more effective way (*www.mayoclinic.org*).

CBT can be effective in treating anxiety, depression, and even certain mental illnesses. This therapy focuses on the present moment and not the past. The goal is to help you identify learned negative thoughts and behaviors through therapy and exercises at home. This will help you unlearn these thoughts and allow you to adopt a healthier way of thinking. It can be taught by psychologists, therapists, psychiatric nurses, and even social workers who have been certified in CBT.

Hormone replacement therapy (HRT) is another option to help alleviate some of your symptoms. A disruption in your hormones can upset the balance of neurotransmitters in your brain, which can exacerbate any anxiety or depression you may be experiencing. Talk with your physician to see if this is an option for you.

Bioidentical Hormone Replacement Therapy (BHRT) is another option you may choose to explore. BHRT uses processed hormones that come from plants. Estrogen, progesterone, and testosterone are the most commonly used bioidentical hormones (*my.clevelandclinic.org*).

Not all BHRT is approved by the FDA. Many alternative physicians can write prescriptions for compounded forms specific to your own personal needs. Many women, including myself, have had great success with this type of therapy. They come in creams, dissolvable pills, and vaginal inserts. As with any medication, vitamin, or supplement, please talk to your physician before starting any new regimen. There may be side-effects and drug contraindications between these and your current medications and any health conditions you may have. Only your physician can make that decision.

Please do not use the internet as a resource. You may receive false information that can be detrimental to your health.

This chapter has a lot of information and suggestions; but the bottom line is for *you* to learn how to effectively communicate with your partner, physician, and loved ones about what you are going through. It may be uncomfortable at first to be honest and open with your feelings, but like all things, practice makes perfect. Communicating your innermost feelings can lead to a healthier and more intimate relationship with your spouse. *And who doesn't want more of that?*

CHAPTER 10

I discovered that when I believed my thoughts I suffered, but when I didn't believe them I didn't suffer, and that this is true for every human being. Freedom is as simple as that. I found that suffering is optional. I found a joy within me that has never disappeared, not for a single moment. That joy is in everyone, always. And I invite you not to believe me. I invite you to test it for yourself.

—BYRON KATIE

YOU'RE STILL SEXY

Sex – I have saved the best for last! As part of my research in writing this book, I reached out to other women: friends, relatives, coworkers, and even acquaintances, to ask them about the physical and mental side effects that they had experienced during menopause. I received the routine answers of hot flashes, weight gain, irritability, fatigue, and sleep issues. I also wondered, "What about their sex drive?" I did not want to ask such a personal question because I thought that nobody would want to answer. Wow, was I wrong!

I went around a second time and asked this very personal question. Most women were more than eager to talk about their sex life during menopause. I was under the assumption that women had lost the drive for intimacy. This was not the case. Many of these women shared that they had an increased sex drive once they overcame all those pesky physical symptoms.

In the beginning of menopause, these women had lost their sex drive. They had gained weight, experienced hot flashes, mood swings and had increased stress and anxiety. Their self-esteem had plummeted, which made them self-conscious in the bedroom. They did not feel sexy to themselves or to their partner. They were not having conversations regarding how they were feeling, which made them feel like they were drifting away from their spouses.

> Many women shared that their sex lives had dramatically improved after menopause.

But once they were able to understand what their bodies were going through, they were able to have a healthy sex life again. Many even shared that their sex lives had dramatically improved after menopause. There was less stress in their lives. Their children were grown and had moved out of the house leaving

CHAPTER 11

more time for intimacy. They didn't have to plan out when they could have sex. They could even leave the door open. How awesome is that! Of course, there was the relief that they could not get pregnant. No planning around their menstrual cycles. No worries about condoms either. There is a freedom knowing that you can have sex anywhere and at any time.

How do you remain sexually active, feel sexy, and enjoy life in menopause? It's not as hard as you think. The first step is communication with your spouse or partner. Sharing your feelings can bring the two of you closer. Ask yourself a few questions. Are you wanting to have more intimacy in your life? What makes you feel and look sexy? Is there an outfit in which you look amazing? If so, wear it more often. Take the time to make yourself look beautiful every day. Fix your hair, put your makeup on, and wear clothes that are flattering on you. When you take pride in how you look, it will boost your self-esteem and help you become closer to your spouse.

When I met my husband, I thought he was the greatest man I had ever met. For the first time in my life, I felt like someone loved me, for *ME*. He paid attention to what I said and even the clothes and jewelry I wore. On holidays and birthdays, he would give me gifts of things that I said I liked months prior. How could he remember those things? "Because I love you," he said. He would give me compliments every day, telling me how beautiful I was and how perfect I was for him. I had low self-esteem and would negate his comments by saying things like, "Stop, I'm not that pretty," or "You only say that because you love me."

Then one day, he came to me and said that he was going to stop giving me compliments because it hurt his feelings – and if I didn't appreciate it then why should he continue? This made me stop and think, *wow, what have I done*? I could not imagine my husband not saying all those wonderful things to me. So, I made a choice right then and there. I would gratefully accept his compliments, whether I believed them or not. I would say thank you and give him a big kiss on the cheek. Before you know it, I started to accept those compliments and stopped doubting my own inner beauty.

So, ask your spouse what he finds sexy in you. Is it the way you style your hair and makeup, a certain outfit you wear, or maybe he loves the way you move your hips when you walk? It may surprise you to hear his answer. Men are not as critical in the way they look at themselves as women are.

CHAPTER 11

We can be brutal to ourselves. I am my own worst enemy when it comes to giving myself compliments. I tend to find all the faults instead of finding my attributes. Trust in what your spouse says, even though it may sound silly to you.

If your husband tells you that he loves it when you are wearing just a t-shirt and underwear, then surprise him one day. Casually come out in that outfit and sit on the couch next to him. I bet his eyes will light up and he will have the biggest smile on his face. It doesn't take much ladies. It just takes effort. Listen to what your partners are saying to you. Men say what they mean. If they tell you something they like, it is a hint for you and can be a great turn-on for them. Reclaiming your sexual prowess can be one of the greatest gifts you can give to yourself, your spouse, and your marriage.

> Reclaiming your sexual prowess can be one of the greatest gifts you can give to yourself, your spouse, and your marriage.

Make your bedroom a sanctuary for sleep and sex. Ditch the photos of the kids, grandparents, and pets. When you are intimate with your spouse, the last thing you want to look up at is your grandma staring at you from the picture frame. Make sure you have beautiful bedding, soft lighting, diffuse oils, and even candles around the room. Candles can help set the mood for romance. They also help to flatter the body in that sexy lingerie you are wearing. You can even play soft music in the background to help set the mood.

When your spouse comes to you with that look in his eye, don't tell him you are not in the mood. By saying an automatic *no*, you don't give yourself a chance to get in the mood. If you are busy, tell him that you will be ready in 30 minutes. This will allow you time to get yourself relaxed and in the mood. Get those candles and essential oils going in the bedroom. Put on your favorite sexy outfit and lay in bed. Allow yourself to relax and just embrace the moment.

Tell your spouse that you want to be intimate, but no sex. This can be a great turn on for both of you – just touch and caress each other. This is also a great time to tell him how much you love and appreciate him. Before you know it, that touching and kissing will turn into something else. What about orgasms? If this has been an issue, tell yourself that you are not striving to have one. Just allow yourself to enjoy the intimacy between the two of you. This will take all the pressure off and allow you to relax even more. In fact, you can make it fun for you and your spouse. Try having sex in the spare bedroom or even on your back patio

CHAPTER 11

– just make sure your neighbors can't see. That could be quite embarrassing. You would be famous in your neighborhood though.

A great way to reconnect with your spouse is going to couple's therapy. Therapists have a great way of allowing couples to communicate in a non-threatening manner. They provide non-judgmental feedback and can give you *sex homework*, which can be fun. A great book to read together is *The 5 Love Languages* by Dr. Gary Chapman. This is a wonderful book on how to express and experience love for each other. There are free resources on their website to help get you started (*5lovelanguages.com*).

They say food is a great way to reach a man's heart. Eating aphrodisiac foods can help as well. These foods can help decrease inflammation in the body, improve vascular tone, and help to balance your hormones. The #1 food most people think of is oysters. There has been some controversy over whether they really do work or not, but men have been eating them for hundreds of years and vouch for their effects on libido. Oysters are high in zinc, which may help with male testosterone levels. Zinc also helps maintain dopamine levels, which science suggests can increase sexual arousal. They are also high in Omega-3, which may increase blood flow and aid erectile and testicular function (*www.healthline.com*).

Many fruits can work as aphrodisiacs as well. Figs and pomegranates are the top two. Figs contain amino acids that help with the production of nitric oxide. This helps to increase blood flow to the genitals by expanding blood vessels, which helps to increase arousal. Pomegranates are touted to help both men and women increase their mood and sex drive. They are packed with antioxidants, which help improve blood circulation to your sex organs. This increase in blood flow helps with erectile dysfunction and can also help lubricate the vaginal walls, making it easier to reach orgasm.

Almonds, brazil nuts, and pine nuts can be helpful as well. They all contain zinc and selenium, which help improve circulation and decrease inflammation. A recent study found that men who added 60 grams – about 1/2 cup – of nuts to their daily diet improved several aspects of their sexual life. The results were published online June 19, 2019, by the journal *Nutrients*. Researchers asked 83 healthy men to follow either a traditional Western-style diet without nuts, or a Western-style diet that also included 60 grams (about 360 calories) of a nut mixture made from almonds,

CHAPTER 11

hazelnuts, and walnuts every day. A questionnaire assessed their current sexual function. After 14 weeks, men in the nut group reported improvement in sexual function like sexual desire, and in the quality of orgasms compared with those in the control group (*www.health.harvard.edu*).

Lastly, we have dark chocolate. Who doesn't love chocolate? It is sold on every corner on Valentine's Day and is given as gifts for holidays and birthdays. The word chocolate symbolizes love, romance, and even sexual pleasure. It contains B vitamins and antioxidants, which help improve circulation and improve inflammation. It is also rich in magnesium, which helps in the production of sex hormones. It also contains phenylethylamine, a compound that acts like a stimulant, and can trigger the same endorphins produced during sex.

If the foot of the trees were not tied to the earth, they would be pursuing me. For I have blossomed so much, I am the envy of the gardens.

—RUMI

12

EMBRACING THE CRONE AND HER WISDOM

I learned a great lesson as a child. I felt privileged to grow up in a small farm town in Ohio. We lived 15 minutes from town, in an isolated, yet comforting farmhouse. Our house was surrounded by corn fields on three sides. In the front yard there was a large maple tree that appeared to have been there for a very long time. The trunk was thick, and the branches were wide and full of leaves flowing from them.

There were no other houses within sight of ours, which meant there were no friends to play with. That did not bother me, though. I learned early on to embrace the quiet solitude of this wonderful place. Across the small road was a forested area where a small creek flowed year-round. I spent my summers in that forest, playing make-believe with all the critters that surrounded me. The little frogs and turtles were my imaginary friends. My dad always had a large vegetable garden. He would come home from work, and we would go out back and pick the day's harvest. I still remember biting into that sun-drenched tomato, warm from the sun. We would take our harvest into the house and prepare it for winter. Some vegetables were eaten for dinner that night, the others were either canned or frozen for use later. "We have to be prepared for the colder months ahead," my dad would say to me. As a child, I didn't quite understand what he meant. I can now look back and appreciate what he taught me. I carry these fond memories with me every day.

I learned as a child that life is like the seasons. We start our life as spring: young, fresh, and beautiful. Some cultures call this the *maiden stage*. This is the time where we need to be nurtured, like a seedling planted in the ground, filling our roots with the nutrients of life – such as knowledge, patience, love, and compassion. We are focused on ourselves. This is when we go to school, make friends, and

CHAPTER 12

learn right from wrong. We are driven and maybe even competitive. We can accomplish a lot with all that energy – we are learning the essence of life.

Then we go off to college, start our career, and meet the love of our life. We get married and have children along with a dog and two cats, maybe even a goldfish. We spend the next 20 years in the summer of our life, the *mother stage*. We are strong mentally, physically, and emotionally. We are independent – in the prime of our life. We nurture new life, and it is no longer just about ourselves. Most of us are not thinking about getting older. We save our money for retirement, but we don't really think about who we will be when we are older. We cannot imagine losing our youth.

Time goes on, our children get older, go to college, and start to form their own adult life. Then, one day you look in the mirror and you see this different version of yourself. It's you, but you have started to age. How did this happen? It feels like it happened overnight. You were so busy tending to your summer garden that you forgot about the fall.

The fall of your life is finally here. You may feel lost and confused. This is called your *guardian stage*. You start to notice fine lines on your face, more gray hair on your head, and a few extra pounds on your body each year. You may try and fight it every step of the way. You may look for the fountain of youth in every jar of face cream and every box of hair dye. You may find that you are feeling more anxious and stressed out. You struggle each day, just as most women do in our culture. We push through the aches and pains and ignore the signs of stress. We blame our jobs, our lack of time, our spouses, just about everything else we can think of.

What if, instead, you embrace the blessings of the *crone*. The *stage of the crone* is a time of heightened awareness of human nature and allows you to acknowledge and honor the wisdom, experience, and resilience that comes with age.

After menopause, you will have more knowledge, wisdom and experience than ever before!

Once menopause is over, you will no longer be so emotional. For the first time in your adult life, you will no longer have monthly hormonal fluctuations. You will no longer have cycles or bleed each month. This brings stability and consistency to life. You will have more knowledge, wisdom and experience than ever before! You are powerful and can calm those around you.

CHAPTER 12

Over time, you start to accept the change of the seasons. You finally realize that you are in the fall of your life. You are now determined to be prepared for winter. You recover from the busy summer and over time, you learn to embrace this season of life. You allow yourself to become selfish, taking more time for yourself and not feeling guilty for it. You take long walks in the forest, watching the leaves sway gently with the soft, cool breeze. The leaves are vibrant in color, looking more beautiful than before. You soon realize that you, too, are changing with the leaves.

> You are changing like the leaves do in fall.

At this stage, I feel more confident in myself than ever before. I tell myself that I am beautiful, inside and out. This time of my life – this season – is becoming the best time of my life. I am now preparing myself for the changing of the season. This new season of my life will be entering winter in a few years. I am no longer afraid of this transition. I have a lifetime of love, laughter, and knowledge that will sustain me during this time. I look forward to my leaves falling off the branches. I will continue to stand tall, year after year, enduring the cold and the bitterness that those before me have foretold. But is this so? It may be for some, but others have flourished during this stage of life.

SOLVING THE MYSTERY OF MENOPAUSE

Women's experience of menopause is highly influenced by cultural attitudes and beliefs towards menopause and menopausal symptoms (*www.continence.org.au*). In western culture, many view menopause as an end – an end to fertility, youth, and sexual vitality. The only preparation women have is to dread this time of their life.

Why do our elders hide this time of their life and treat it as an embarrassment? I found it difficult to find adequate information on the subject when writing this chapter. Over time, our families have grown apart. We are not as close-knit as generations before us. When I was a child, we would spend the weekends and the summers with our families. We would have barbecues, go camping, and even go to the lake. Every Thanksgiving, our family would drive hundreds of miles to get to our house, just so we could be together at this special time.

> Cultures outside of the western world have a healthier view of menopause and aging.

The elder women would be in the kitchen cooking, the men watching football. The children were outside playing and sneaking into the kitchen to steal food from the counter. But not me. I wanted to be in the kitchen with all my elders. I loved hearing them talk about their childhood and relatives that had long been gone. They would laugh and sometimes cry. You could feel the love and energy in that kitchen.

As I got older, the family gatherings started slowing down. People got busier and moved farther away. The elders, who once insisted on these gatherings, were slowly passing away, taking the family traditions with them. The young women of this generation no longer have someone to look up to. The once intact family unit has disappeared in this part of the world.

Many other cultures throughout the world still adopt the concept of multigenerational families. Three generations living under one roof – grandparents, parents, and children. Each generation learning from the other increases the bonds that form between them. Perhaps that is why cultures outside of the western world have a healthier view of menopause and aging.

> The *wise one* is fierce and radiates confidence.

Many cultures view postmenopausal women as being strong and powerful. They refer to these women as *Elders*, or *The Crone* of the family. The younger generations look up to her, as she is filled with an inner confidence. *The Wise One* is fierce and radiates confidence. Many of these women are leaders in their community and are considered extremely powerful. A common belief among traditional shamanic cultures – for example, Mayan women and the Cree women of Canada – is that women must enter menopause to access their shamanic and healing powers. Menstrual blood has the power to create life in the womb, so when women reach the age of retaining their *wise blood*, they cross the threshold into *wise womanhood* by keeping their wise blood within. At this point they become priestesses and healers – the spiritual leaders of their communities (*www.womenshealthnetwork.com*).

The Japanese do not have a word for hot flashes and consider this time in a woman's life to be a transition, rather than viewed as a loss. Native Americans do not have a word for menopause in their native language and their tribe considers them to be wise women, often giving them more power in decision making in the community.

These are just a few of the differences in cultural views on menopause. No matter what part of the world you live in, or what you were led to believe, menopause should be viewed as a natural process. Almost every woman will experience menopause. The only exceptions are those adolescents that have had their ovaries removed before they experience puberty.

CHAPTER 12

To fully embrace this time of our life, we must first allow ourselves to change, mentally and physically. We need to educate ourselves so that this transition will flow easily, like waves in the ocean. There will be good days and bad days, but early mental preparation will help you to find strength and peace during this season of your life.

It is a time of transformation. Just like a caterpillar that morphs into a butterfly. You are shedding your past, only to become beautiful, magnificent, and free flowing. You are changing with the seasons. Unlike the butterfly, this transformation does not take place over weeks, but over years of knowledge and personal growth. We must discard the old ways of thinking and allow ourselves to be reborn. We have a responsibility not only to ourselves, but to our children and the younger generation of women that will be taking our place in the future.

Menopause starts in your 50s. The life expectancy of women today is approximately 79.1 years per the CDC (*www.cdc.gov*). This means that you have 30 wonderful years to live the best life possible. This should be viewed as a beginning, not an end. Embrace every aspect of your life. Stop and smell the flowers. Sleep in, take afternoon naps, walk barefoot in your garden. You can do anything that you want to do during this amazing time. Now is the time to travel the world, volunteer, or just simply sit and read a book.

I hope this book has inspired you to take charge of your life. It is the beginning of a bright new future. Look forward to the changing of the seasons as they bring forth hope and new possibilities. Reflect on the past and embrace the potential of the future. Life moves on with or without us, so why not take a seat and enjoy the ride.

> *You're off to Great Places! Today is your day!*
> *Your mountain is waiting, So... get on your way!*
> —DR. SEUSS, *OH, THE PLACES YOU'LL GO!*

CHAPTER 12

These principles provide a holistic approach to navigating menopause, addressing various aspects of physical, emotional, and mental well-being. Here's a brief overview of each principle:

Twelve Principles to Navigate Menopause
1. Face the Truth
2. Build a Team
3. Talk about It
4. Have Fun
5. Educate Yourself
6. Manage Your Symptoms
7. Love Your Gut
8. Pamper Yourself
9. Calm Yourself
10. Cultivate Sanity
11. Embrace Your Changing Sexuality
12. Celebrate

ACKNOWLEDGMENTS

First and foremost, I would like to thank my patient husband Jay. He has put up with my ever changing mood swings over the past few years and yet, still adores me.

I would not be the woman I am today without the love and support of the many wise women in my life. They have always been there for me and helped mold me into the strong woman I am today. I am fortunate to call them mother, aunt, and cousin.

I'd like to give a shout-out to the team at O'Leary Publishing for making this book possible. I am grateful to April and Heather for being patient with me and guiding me through this unchartered territory.

I would also like to thank Dr. Amber Passini. Without her knowledge and guidance, I would be a hormonal mess!

ABOUT THE AUTHOR

Angela Martinez, an Ohio native, now lives with her husband and three cats in the mountains of South Carolina. She enjoys gardening, cooking, and traveling. She admits to being a self-care junkie and loves to pamper herself. She has a passionate and adventurous spirit that led her to work for the airlines, which allowed her quest for travel to take her around the globe. She has an unwavering passion to guide people on their journey to a healthier lifestyle and a desire to see others thrive. On her quest for knowledge in achieving optimal health, she became a massage therapist, a reiki II practitioner, and a certified health and wellness coach. She is now a registered nurse who specializes in psychiatric nursing.